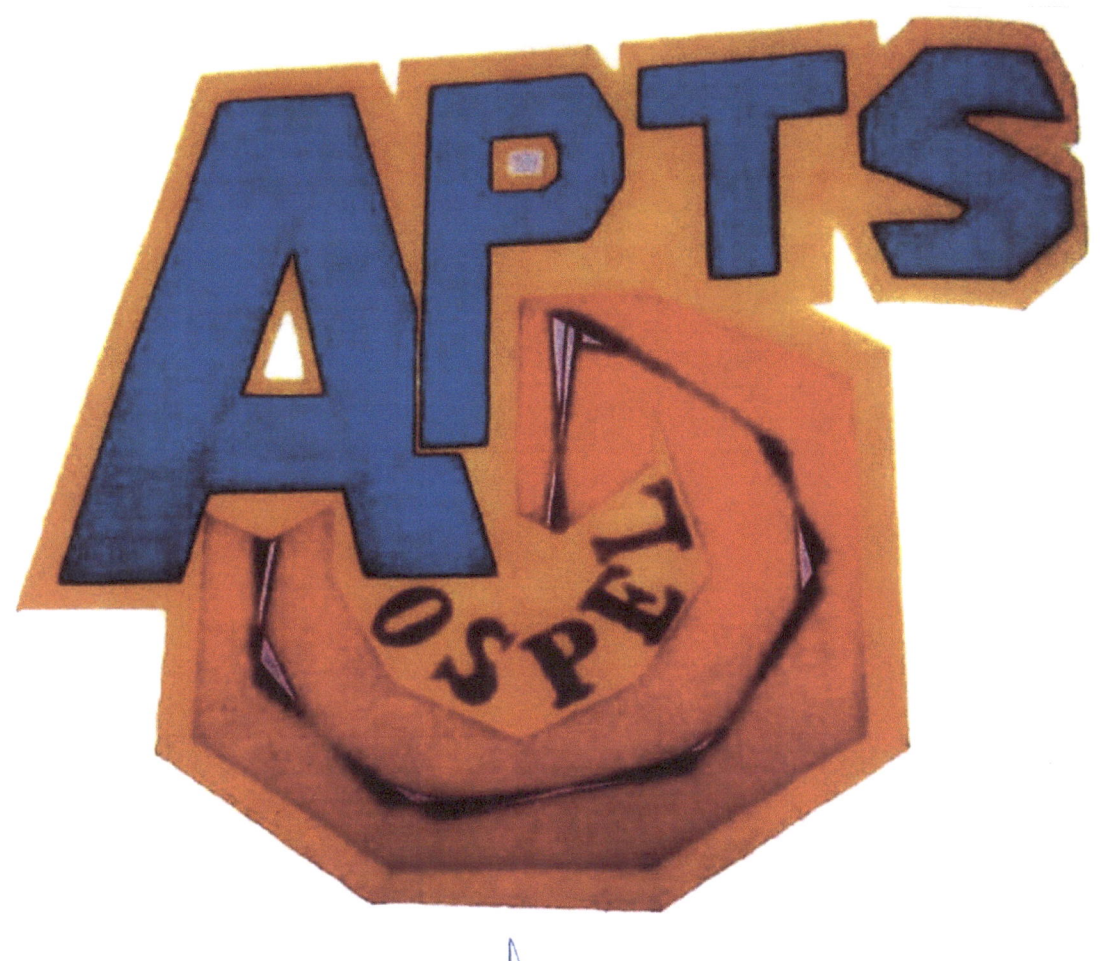

TAARIQ "R—I—Q" JAAMAL

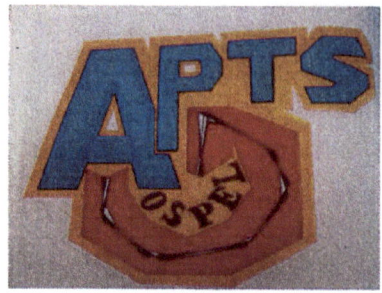

Copyright © 2025 by Taariq Jaamal

Authority, God placed it on every Born Again Spirit

Printed in the United States of America

ISBN 9798218740368

All rights reserved sold by the author. The author guarantees all contents are original and do not infringe upon the legal rights of any other person or works.

Unless otherwise indicated, Scripture quotations are taken from King James Version (KJV) - public domain.

Book Designer: Taariq Jaamal

Book front cover Designer: Winifred Billington, Simply Winnie, LLC.

Book back cover Designer: Taariq Jaamal

Copy Editor: R-I-Q, The Lyrical Minister

If you have any questions or comments concerning this book, please write or contact:

GospelApts Publishing/ Taariq Jaamal

GospelApts Readers Service

TheReceipt2K15Authority2K25@gmail.com

Windsor, CT. 06095

Library of Congress Control Number: 2025915031

The GospelApts book on Authority, God placed it on every Born Again Spirit mission is to empower people's lives with the knowledge, wisdom and understanding of the power of God's given Authority to man. Taking Authority, exercising and releasing authority IN THE NAME OF JESUS. This book includes exercises on how to use your authority for your children, family, friends, associates, neighbors, enemies and yourself. Defeating Satan, demon and evil spirits, and all wickedness of the world IN THE NAME OF JESUS.

N GOD RIQ TRUST
Introduction: RIQZ Prayer
Written by Taariq "R-I-Q" Jaamal

Heavenly Father,
In Jesus name,
I thank you for blessing me to be here another day.
and God's Will, many more days, weeks, months and years of the Blessed Life.
Father, I am thankful for my life, health, wealth, strength, power and authority
that you place on my life today,
and all the things I am able and blessed to do today.
God, you are my number one priority,
I want to fulfill your will and complete
all that it is you want me to do today, God.
Father, You are my source and supply
and I call on you in Jesus name
for all of my needs, my wants and desires of my heart
pertaining to life and godliness and knowing.
God, I thank you for the blessings,
Jesus, I thank you for the healing,
Holyspirit, I thank you for the guidance,
Angels, I thank you for the protection,
and God,
I thank you for the wisdom I have
to operate in all the cares of my life today,
Jesus Christ who did it all.

Jesus, thank you for doing it all

Thank you Jesus for healing me.
Jesus, you are my Lord and savior,
my big brother, my joint heir,
you are my everything,
you are my wisdom,
Jesus, I believe in you.
Jesus, I have faith in you.
Jesus, I trust in you.
I walk with you Jesus,
I talk to you Jesus,
I pray through you Jesus,
I follow you Jesus,
I love you Jesus,
thank you Jesus for doing it all
and all glory be to God,
In Jesus name.

Holy spirit, thank you for the guidance

Holy Spirit, I thank you for guiding me,
You are my best friend that dwells within
and abides with me forever.
I thank you for guiding me in all truths
and showing me right from wrong
and lining me up with the word of God.
Preaching, teaching and speaking
the gospel Grace to me,
uplifting me and letting me know
what it is that God wants me to do today.
Thank you for praying with me,
through me and for me.
Thank you for leading, directing and coaching me,
as you guide me in all truths.
Holy Spirit, I pray for my ears, eyes and mouth gates
to be open that i may recognize your voice,
understand what you're guiding me through
and what it is God wants me to do today.
Holy spirit, I thank you for the spiritual guidance
And I love you.

Angels, thank you for the protection

Angels, my friends forever,
I thank you and love you

Angels,
I thank you for protecting me,
I thank you for watching over me,
I thank you angels for fighting from victory
To victory on my behalf,
I thank you for covering me with the wings of love
And protecting me from evil every day of my life.

Father, In Jesus name

Father, in Jesus name
I pray for those who will pray
and those who won't pray,
those who love and those who hate,
and father I pray for those who are unable
to pray regardless of their situations or
circumstances.
Father, I pray for all that was here yesterday,
my children, family, friends, associates, neighbors,
enemies and I.
I pray that we are all blessed to be here another day.
God's will, many more days, weeks, months and
years of the Blessed Life.
In Jesus name, God I thank you.

God, In Jesus name

God, in Jesus name,
I asked that you place your hands amongst
each and every one of us today.
Increasing our lives and widening our borders
and writing it on our minds and hearts,
what it is you want us to do today.
God, in Jesus name,
I ask that you protect us as we travel,
however we travel and wherever we may travel to,
that we have no accidents, no breakdowns, no harm
done or casualties.
Father, I pray for a day of love, peace, joy and
happiness and knowing.
Father, protect us from sickness, evil, disease, lack
and poverty,
and not letting evil Hurt nor grieve us,
that we may have victory, success and prosperity
in every arena of our lives today.
In Jesus name, God I thank you.

Thank you for the Blessing

Thank you for the blessings, God.
Thank you for the healing, Jesus.
Thank you for the guidance, Holy Spirit.
Thank you for the protection, Angels.
and God,
I thank you for the wisdom
We all have to operate in all the cares in our lives today.
Father, I thank you for your unmerited favor,
mercy, love, power, strength and Authority,
and your goodness and kindness
that uplifts and leads to repentance.
God, I plead the blood of the lamb,
the blood of Jesus Christ,
to cover us in every Arena of Our Lives today.
In Jesus name, father I thank you.
In the name of the father,
And in the name of the Son,
And in the name of the Holy spirit,
And angels from up above, One Love.

Let us all Pray

Let us all pray,

Our Father,
which art in heaven,
I'll be thy name.
thy kingdom come,
thy will be done in earth,
as it is in heaven.
Give us this day our daily bread.
and forgive us our debts,
as we forgive our debtors.
and lead us not into temptation,
but deliver us from evil;
for thine is the kingdom,
and the Power,
and the Glory,
For ever.
Amen.

N GOD RIQ TRUST   Riqz: Morning Prayer

Heavenly father,
In Jesus name, I thank you for blessing my children, family, friends, associates, neighbors, enemies and I to be here another day.
God's will many more days, weeks, months and years of the Blessed life.
In Jesus name, father I thank you for placing your hands amongst each and every one of us today,
increasing our lives and widening our borders and writing it on our minds and hearts what it is you want us to do today.
Thank you father, for protecting us as we travel,
However we may travel and wherever we may travel to, that we have no accidents, no breakdowns, no harm done or casualties.
Thank you God, for this day of love, peace, joy and happiness….And knowing.
Thank you God for protecting us from sickness, evil, disease, lack and poverty and that we all might have victory, success and prosperity in every Arena of Our Lives today.
In Jesus name, God, I thank you.
Amen.

Authority,
God placed it on every born again spirit.
Exercising Authority.

In Jesus name,
I have authority given to me by God,
and with this power,
I'm taking Authority
and releasing Authority
In the name of Jesus.
Therefore, In the name of Jesus,
I command you Satan,
demon spirits, evil spirits and all wicked tries of the world,
to back away from my children, my family, my friends, my associates,
my neighbors, my enemies and I, right here, right now, in the name of Jesus.
I command you to cease all maneuvers, operations and temptations to steal,
kill and destroy any of us, in the name of Jesus.
Satan, you and all your servants,
I command you to get out of the mind, thoughts and bodies you're controlling and destroying.
I command in the name of Jesus,

Satan and all your servants to flee and get out of the mind, thoughts and bodies of my children, my family, my friends, my associates, my neighbors, my enemies and I, right here, right now,
In the name of Jesus,
I'm not asking, begging or arguing,
I command in the name of Jesus,
be gone in the name of Jesus,
I command you to flee and leave the minds, thoughts and bodies
you're controller and destroying, it stops right here, right now in the name of Jesus,
In the name of Jesus,
In the name of Jesus,
In the name of Jesus,
In the name of Jesus,
In the name of Jesus,
In the name of Jesus,
It is done,
I release my authority,
In the name of Jesus,
glory be to God,
And thank you Jesus.

AUTHORITY

Repent:
Re- pent /re- pent/
verb.

1. Feel or express sincere regret or remorse about one's wrongdoing or sin.
    "The priest urged his listeners to repent" synonyms: feel remorse, regret, be sorry, rue, reproach oneself, be ashamed, feel contrite,
    more be penitent, be remorseful, be repentant. "The President claims
    to have repented."
2. View or think of (an action or omission) with deep regrets or remorse. "Michelle came to repent her nasty judgment." archaic- feel regret or penitence about " I repent me of all i did"

Repent (KJV)
 To change one's mind and purpose; repent to have a change of mind and heart.
From that time Jesus began to preach, and say, REPENT: for the kingdom of heaven is at hand Matthew 4: 17

AUTHORITY

Repent

To lament one's action: turn again

And God saw that the wickedness of man was great in the Earth, and that every imagination of the thoughts of his heart was only evil continually. And it REPENTED the LORD that he had made man of the Earth, and it grieved him at his heart.
Genesis 6: 5-6

Man can not and will never become righteous by his goodness, Good Deeds, kindness, on performance, wealth and self-efforts.

Man must come to an end of himself and realize he needs a Lord and Savior.

R-I-Q, Jesus loves me
and we love you too.

Man, woman and children,
I pray for you all to "call on the Lord".

AUTHORITY
REPENTANCE:

If you do this I believe and declare your life will be forever changed. Make Jesus the Lord of your life. Pray for repentance, choose one of these prayers with hope, faith and belief, inviting Jesus Christ into every area of your life.

Prayer one:
Lord Jesus, I come to an end of myself,
I Repent of all my sins,
Jesus, come into my heart,
I call On you Lord,
for healing and salvation,
I'll make you my Lord and Savior,
Thank you Jesus.

Prayer two:
Lord Jesus, I asked for forgiveness
of my sins Lord,
cleanse me of all sins,
come into my life Lord,
I call On You Jesus to sit on the throne of my heart,
and be my Lord and Savior,
Thank you Jesus.

If you prayed one of these prayers in belief, I believe you're a New Covenant born again Christian. You're blessed by God, healed by Jesus Christ, guided by the Holyspirit in all truths and protected by the angels from evil.

AUTHORITY

God said:
I Will- I Will- I Will

Be Your God

God said:
Authority,
Is in every Born again Spirit,
"you are a child of the most high God"

The authority,
God has already provided his healing,
power and placed it on the inside of every Born again believer. It is up to us to use it.

Understanding and using our Authority is the master key to seeing miracles happen.

AUTHORITY

Born again with Authority
*God-given Authority
* Grace given Authority

I am the righteousness of God through the perfect finished works of Jesus Christ by faith.

Jesus' Authority has been given to us.

And Jesus came and spoke to them, saying, all authority has been given to me in heaven and on earth. Go ye therefore, and teach All nations, baptizing them in the name of the father, and the son, and the Holy Ghost. Teaching them to observe all things whatsoever I have commanded you; and, lo, I am with you always [Even] unto the end of the world.

Matthew 28: 18- 19

Let every person be subject to the governing authorities. for there is no Authority except from God, and those that exist have been instituted by God.

Romans: 13:1

Behold, I have given you Authority to tread on serpents and scorpions and over all the power of the enemy, and nothing shall hurt you.

Luke 10:19

For the Lord God is a sun and shield; the Lord bestows favor and honor. No good thing does he withhold from those who walk upright.
Psalms 84:11

AUTHORITY

Born again with Authority

Jesus defeated Satan, taking the sting out of death and the Authority he had stolen from man. Authority over all the abilities of the adversary. Every bornagain spirit is sealed with authority over all the abilities of Satan and his servants, all evils.

Jesus- he did it all,

That we who believe in him be made righteous, righteous by God.
He achieves all that we may need, want and the desires of our hearts pertaining to life and godliness.
Believe and receive what Jesus achieved. Partake in Jesus Christ,
Say- I partake in Jesus Christ.

Born again Christians,
By the God- given Authority,
Grace- giving Authority invested in you.

Take authority- In the name of Jesus
Release Authority- In the name of Jesus
Exercise Authority- In the name of Jesus
And make use of your Authority in the name of Jesus

Commanding Satan and all evils to cease and stop all maneuvers, operations, and temptations against you and other people's lives.
Right now, Right here- In the name of Jesus.

AUTHORITY

Christ, when tempted by Satan, answered him with scripture.

Matthew 4:1-11

Then Jesus let up of the Spirit Into the Wilderness to be tempted of the devil. 2 And when he had fasted 40 days and 40 nights, he was afterward an hungred. 3 And when the temperature came to him, he said, if thou be the son of God, command that these Stones be made bread. 4 but he answered and said, it is written, man shall not live by bread alone, but by the every word that precedeth out of the mouth of God.5 Then the devil taketh him up into the holy city, and setteth him on a pinnacle of the Temple,6 And saith unto him, if thou be the son of God, cast thyself down: for it is written, he shall give his angels charge concerning thee: and in their hands they shall bear thee up, lest at any time thou dash thy foot against a stone.7 Jesus said unto him, It is written again, Thou shalt not tempt the Lord thy God.8 Again, the devil taketh him up into an exceeding high mountain, and sheweth him all the kingdoms of the world, and the glory of them.9 And saith unto him, all these things will I give thee, if thou will fall down and worship me.10 Then saith Jesus until him, get thee hence, Satan: for it is written, thou shalt Worship the Lord thy God, and him only shalt thou serve.11 Then the devil leaveth him, and, behold, angels came and ministered unto him.

AUTHORITY

God has given us his full armour to stand against evil, it is not necessary for Christians to rebuke Satan.

Ephesians 6: 10-18
10 Finally, my brethren, be strong in the Lord, and in the power of his might 11 Put on the whole armor of God, that ye may be able to stand against the wiles of the devil.12 For we wrestle not against flesh and blood, but against principalities, against powers, against the rules of the darkness of the world, against spiritual wickedness in high places.13 Wherefore taken unto you the whole armour of God, that ye may be able to withstand in the evil day, and having done all, to stand.14 Stand therefore, having your Loins girt about with truth, and having on the breastplate of righteousness;15 And your feet shod with the preparation of the gospel of peace; 16 Above all, take the shield of faith, wherewith ye shall be able to quench all the fiery darts of the wicked.17 And take the helmet of salvation, and the sword of the Spirit, which is the word of God.18 Praying always with all prayer and supplication in the spirit and watching thee unto with all perseverance and supplication for all Saints.

AUTHORITY

SCRIPTURES

Take unto you the whole armour of God,
Stand therefore,

Having:
- Your Loins girt about with truths
- Breastplate of Righteousness
- Your feet shod with preparation of the gospel of peace

Take:
- The Shield of faith, quench all fiery darts of the wicked
- The Helmet of Salvation
- The Sword of the Spirit which is the Word of God

2 Corinthians: 10:3-5
3 For though we walk in the flesh, we do not war after the flesh. 4 (for the weapons of our Warfare are not carnal, but Mighty through God to the pulling down of strongholds;) 5 Casting down imaginations, and every high thing that exalteth itself against the knowledge of God, and bringing into captivity every thought to the Obedience of Christ;

AUTHORITY

SCRIPTURES

Ephesians 2:2
Where in in time past ye walked according to the course of this world, according to the prince of the power of the air, the spirit that now worketh in the children of disobedience:

Those who are not under the control of the Sovereign God, are under the control of the devil.

1 Peter 5:8
Be sober, be vigilant; because your adversary the devil, as a roaring lion, walking about, seeking whom he may devour:

Satan is the power at work in the hearts of those who refuse to obey God.

2 Corinthians 4:4
In whom the god of the world hath blinded the minds of them which believe not, lest the light of the glorious gospel of Christ, who is the image of God, should shine unto them.

Acts 26:18
To open their eyes, and to turn them from darkness to light, and from the power of Satan unto God, that they may receive forgiveness of sins, and inheritance among them which are sanctified by faith that is in me.

Born again Christians are no longer enslaved to Satan or to sin.

AUTHORITY

SCRIPTURES

James 4:7
Submit yourselves therefore to God. Resist the devil, and he will flee from you.
The Bible does not give Christians the authority to rebuke the devil, but to resist him.

Romans 6:6-7
knowing this, that our old man is crucified with him, that the body of sin might be destroyed, that henceforth we should not serve sin. 7 For he that is dead is freed from sin.

This does not mean we are immune to the temptations that he, Satan and the adversaries and the devil, puts before us.

Jude 1:9
Yet Mi'-cha-el the archangel, when contending with the devil he disputed about the body of Moses, durst not against him a railing accusation, but said, The Lord rebuke thee.

In response to Satan's attacks, a christian should appeal to Christ. Instead of focusing on defeating the devil, we should focus on following Christ and trust that he will defeat the forces of evil.

Hebrews 12:2
Looking unto Jesus the author and finisher of our faith; Who for the joy that was set before him endured the cross, despising the shame, and is set down at the right hand of the Throne of God.

AUTHORITY

FAITH- What is faith? faith/ fa th/ noun.

1. Complete trust or confidence in someone or something. "this restores one's faith in politicians"

synonym: Trust, belief, confidence, conviction; more.

2. Strong belief in God or in the doctrines of a religion, based on spiritual apprehension rather than proof.

synonyms: religion, Church sect denomination (religious), persuasion(religious), belief, ideology, Creed, teaching, Doctrine.

"she gave her life for her faith"

Faith: Belief, Trust, and loyalty to a person or thing. Christians find their security and hope in God as revealed in Jesus Christ, and say "Amen" to that unique relationship to God in the Holy Spirit through love and obedience as expressed in lives of discipleship and service. Faith:

Hebrews 11:1

Now Faith is the substance of things hoped for, the evidence of things not seen.

Galatians 3:26

We switch from the devil's family to God when we receive Christ by faith; For ye are all the children of God by faith in Christ Jesus.

That's why we major in having faith in Christ.

But there are further blessings when you understand, and trust in, the faith of Christ.

God's order: A Believer's righteousness comes through the Faith of Christ, the righteousness which is of God by faith.

AUTHORITY

PRAISE-What is Praise? Praise/ pr az/ verb.
1. Express warm approval or admiration of.
" we can't praise Taariq enough- he did a brilliant job"
Synonyms: command, applaud, eulogize, compliment, congratulate and admire; more.
Noun.
2. The expression of approval or admiration for someone or something.
"the audience was full of praise for the whole production"
Synonyms: approval, acclimation, admiration, approbation, acclamation, congratulations, commendations; more.
3. The offering of a grateful homage in words or song, as an act of worship: I am a hymn of praise to God.
Praise: A definition of Christian praise is the joyful thinking and adoring of God, the celebrations of his goodness and Grace. This simply implies that the act of praising is rightfully due to God alone.
Praising God- why? The reasons are countless. First, God deserves to be praised and he is worthy to receive our praise. Second, praising God is useful and favorable for us. By praising God, we are reminded of the greatness of God. His power and presence in our lives is reinforced in our understanding. "Praise the Lord, for the Lord is good; sing praise to his name, for that is Pleasant". Third, praising discharges strength and faith, which causes God to move on our behalf. "From the lips of children and infants you have ordained praise because of your enemies, to silence the foes and avenger". Praising God also transforms the spiritual environment that we have. Fourth, God inhabits the atmosphere of praise. says" But thou are Holy, O thou that inhabitest the praise of Israel. If we want to see a clear manifestation of God's blessings and grace, all we need to do is to praise him with all our heart, our mind, and our soul.

AUTHORITY
PRAISE: PRAISING GOD- Who and When?
Who is to Praise God?

Psalm 150:6
Let everything that hath breath praise the Lord. Praise ye the Lord.
I will bless the Lord at all times; his praise will always be on my lips.
Praise the Lord, are you Servants of the Lord who Minister by night in the house of the Lord. lift up your hands and sanctuary and praise the Lord.

Psalm 34:1
I will bless the LORD at all times: his praise shall continually be in my mouth.

Psalm 63:3-4
Because thy lovingkindness is better than life, my lips shall praise thee. Thus will I bless thee while I live.

Psalm 134:1-3
BEHOLD, BLESS ye the Lord, all ye servants of the Lord, which by night in the house of the Lord. lift up your hands in the sanctuary, and bless the Lord. the Lord made heaven and earth bless thee out of zion.

I Corinthians 6: 19-20
What? Know ye not that your body is the temple of the Holy Ghost which is in you, which ye have of God, and ye are not your own? For ye are bought with a price: therefore glorify God in your body, and in your spirit, which are God's. We cannot embark on the true joy and benefits of praising God unless we have received Jesus Christ as our Lord and Savior. As children of God, he dwells in our bodies through the Holy Spirit. This means that wherever we go, God is to Praise. Do you know that your body is a temple of the Holy Spirit, who is in you, whom you have received from God? You are not your own; you were bought at a price. Therefore honor God with your body.

AUTHORITY
PRAISE
WHAT IS PRAISE?

Praise /pr a z/
Verb
1. Express warm approval or admiration of, " we can't praise Taariq enough he did a brilliant job" synonyms: command, applaud, eulogize, compliment, congratulate and admire; more.

Noun
2. The expression of approval or admiration for someone or something, " the audience was full of praise for the whole production", synonyms: approval, acclaim. Admiration, approbation, acclamation, congratulations, commendation; more.
3. The offering of grateful homage in words or songs, as an act of worship: " a hymn of praise to God".

Praise:
A definition of christian praise is the joyful thanking and adoring of God, the celebration of this goodness and grace. This simply implies that the act of praising is rightfully due to God alone.

Praising God- Why? The reasons are countless. First, God deserves to be praised and he is worthy to receive our praise.

Second, praising God is useful and favorable for us. By praising God, we are reminded of the greatness of God! His power and presence in our lives is reinforced in our understanding. "Praise the Lord, for the Lord is good; Sing praise to his name, for that is pleasant (Psalm 135:3).

Third, praising discharges strength in faith, which causes God to move on our behalf, "From the lips of children and infants you have ordained praise because of your enemies, to silence the foe and the avenger" (Psalm 8:2. Praising God also transforms the spirit environment that we have.

Fourth, God inhabits the atmosphere of praise. Psalm 22:3 says "but thou are holy, O thou that inhabitest the praise of Israel!" (KJV). If we want to see a clear manifestation of God's blessings and grace, all we need to do is to praise Him with all our heart, our mind, and our soul.

AUTHORITY

PRAISE

Praising God- Who and When?
Who is to praise God?

" Let everything that has breath praise the LORD, praise the LORD," states Psalm 150:6

"I will bless the LORD at all times; his praise will always be on my lips" (Psalm 34:1)

"Because your love is better than life, my lips will glorify you. I will praise you as long as I live, and in your name I will lift my hands" (Psalm 63:3-4)

Praise the LORD, all you servants of the LORD who minister by night in the house of the LORD. Lift up your hands in sanctuary and praise the LORD" (Psalm 134:1-2).

We can't embark on the true joy and benefits of praising God unless we have received Jesus Christ as our Lord and Savior. As children of God, He dwells in our bodies through the Holy Spirit. This means that wherever we go, God is to be praised.

" Do you know your body is a temple of the Holy Spirit, who is in you, whom you have received from God?
You are not your own; you were bought at a price. Therefore, "Honor God with your body". (Corinthians 6:19-20)

AUTHORITY

CONTENT

A. Authority- The Blessings
1. Authority by God to mankind, God-given authority
2. Power and Strength
3. Understanding power and authority
4. Power of the Holy Spirit
5. Authority Is
6. Christ, grace- given authority
7. Taking authority
8. Speaking authority
9. Speaking with authority
10. Live and walk in this power and authority
11. The physical realm
12. The spiritual realm
13. Spiritual realm characteristics in the physical realm
14. Immutable characteristics
15. The consensus characteristics
16. Physical is, definition
17. Realm is, definition
18. Spiritual is, definition

AUTHORITY

CONTENT

DEMONSTRATIONS

B. Ministering healing and serving
- Into your life
- Into other people lives

"In The Name Of Jesus"

Section 1. Taking Authority
- 1. Eye sight
  - a. Regaining eye sight
  - b. Clear vision restored
  - c. Eyes be healed
- 2. Ears
  - a. Regaining hearing
  - b. Ears to hear
  - c. Hearing be healed

Section 2. Authority over pain in the body
- 1. Pain in the body
  - a. Leave my body
  - b. Leave his and her body
- 2. Cease all pains in the body
  - a. Pain stop and go
  - b. His, her and my pain
  - c. Completely healed
  - d. Body 100% pain free

Section 3. Authority over skin disease
- 1. Speak to heal
  - a. Speak to the body
  - b. Speak to the skin
  - c. Speak to the skin disease
- 2. Body and skin disease
  - a. Skin clear up
  - b. Be disease free
  - c. I call you healed

Section 4. Authority over sickness, diseases and inflammation
- 1. Sickness, disease and inflammation
  - a. Knees
  - b. Body
  - c. The cellular part of the body
- 2. Healing sickness, disease and inflammation
  - a. For every pain- be gone
  - b. Inflammation- be gone
  - c. Knees- be gone

Section 5. Authority over pain in the human body and joints
- 1. Pain in the ligaments
  - a. Knees, hands, feet, ankles, hips, elbows and shoulder pain
  - b. All joints be healed
  - c. ligaments pain free

Section 6. Authority over mind and thoughts
- 1. Speak to your mind and thoughts
  - a. Depression, stress and suicidal thoughts
  - b. Worries, cares and fears
- 2. Healing your mind and thoughts
  - a. Depression, stress and suicidal thoughts
  - b. Worries, cares and fears

Section 7. Authority over the failure of organs in the human body
- 1. The failure of organs in the body
  - a. Heart, lungs, kidney, liver, pancreas and whatever failure lies in the body
  - b. Organs complication
- 2. Healing the organs in the body
  - a. Heart, lungs, kidneys, liver, pancreas and whatever failure lies in the body
  - b. Failure be gone
  - c. Organs be healed
  - d. Restoration

AUTHORITY

CONTENT

Section 8. Authority over LACK and POVERTY
- 1. Lack and poverty in your life
  - a. Food, clothing, shelter, education, healthcare, employment, transportation and anything else you lack in your life
  - b. Needs, wants and desires of the heart pertaining to life and godliness
- 2. Healed, free from lack and poverty in your life
- 3. The lack and poverty leaving your life
  - a. Regaining all that you've lack in your life
  - b. Restoring all that was stolen from you in your life
- 4. Overflowing in abundance
  - a. Needs, wants and desires of the heart
  - b. Pertaining to life and godliness
  - c. Lack and poverty forever leaving your life

Section 9. Authority over demons and evil spirits in the human body
- 1. Evicting all evils out of my life, your life: body
  - a. All demons and evil spirits
  - b. Get out of my mind and thoughts
  - c. Cease all temptations to rent space- body
  - d. Cease satan and all evils
- 2. Evicting all evils out of other people lives
  - a. All demons and evil spirits
  - b. Get out of his and her minds and thoughts
  - c. Cease all temptations to rent space in their bodies
  - d. Cease satan and all evils
- 3. Eviction, casting out satan and all evils
  "In the name of Jesus"

AUTHORITY

CONTENT

Section 10. Authority over cancer in the human body

1. Relieving cancer in the body
   a. Breast, brain, colon, prostate,
      bones and any part of the body
   b. Cancer, leave my body
   c. Cease all operations in my body
   d. Cancer, stop and go
2. Relieving cancer out of other people lives
   a. Breast, brain, colon, prostate
      bones and any part of their body
   b. Cancer, leave his and her body
   c. Cease all operations in their body
   d. Completely healed from cancer

Section 11. Authority over all the abilities of the enemy,
Releasing your authority and power ceasing satan,
demon spirits, evil spirits and all evils

1. All operations, maneuvers and temptations towards
   Your family, friends, foes, and all that you know and love
   And yourself
   a. Get out of my life
   b. Get out of their lives
   c. Cease all attacks

2. Cease all operations, maneuvers and temptations against
   All we know and love
   a. Grandparents, parents, children, aunts, uncles, nieces,
      Nephews and cousins
   b. Added family members, In-laws and their family
   c. Neighbors and communities
   d. The just and unjust

A.
AUTHORITY- THE BLESSINGS

AUTHORITY BY GOD TO MANKIND,
God - given authority
By God to mankind
God loves all his children equal
No more- No less
Believe the word of God, the truth

God's desire is that all his children on earth come to an end of themselves to repentance and be healed. God's will doesn't automatically come to pass. Believe God is God and Jesus is his only begotten son, our lord and savior. Have a change of mind and heart and call on the lord, ask for forgiveness of your sins and welcome Jesus into your life to be your lord and savior. Jesus is the way, the truth and the life, our guiding light.

A new covenant born again christian made righteous by God through the perfect finished works of Jesus Christ by faith, your faith in Christ. Jesus is the one and only way to salvation. With Jesus sitting on the throne of your heart you'll inherit blessings, healings, guidance, protection and eternal life.

GOD LOVES
ALL HIS CHILDREN
EQUAL
NO MORE
NO LESS

AUTHORITY- THE BLESSINGS

2. AUTHORITY: POWER AND STRENGTH,
God - given authority and Grace- given authority
We've got the power and strength

Ministering healing and serving into your life

Minister everything God has made available to you, the word of God and authority. Invest time in the word of God daily renewing your mind. Receive the knowledge, wisdom, and understanding of the word. Read, study, learn, write, speak, teach and meditate on the word of God. It is written, man has power, strength and authority given to us by God and the right to use it, authorized by God. Believe and receive your God - given authority and make use of it, exercise authority.

Most importantly, we have authority over all the abilities of the enemy, the adversary. Satan and his servants want to steal, kill and destroy man. Satan and his servants use philosophy, maneuvers, operations and temptations to prevent you from hearing and believing the word of God. Remember you have the authority to stop the adversary every temptation. Command Satan and all evils to cease everything right now, "In the name of Jesus" by the power invested in you through the perfect finished works of Jesus Christ, release your authority in the name above all names.

RELEASE YOUR AUTHORITY "IN THE NAME OF JESUS CHRIST"

AUTHORITY- THE BLESSINGS

3. UNDERSTANDING POWER AND AUTHORITY

POWER IS THE RAW ABILITY TO DO SOMETHING

POWER WITHOUT AUTHORITY IS ABUSE
ABUSE is to use wrongly or improperly; misuse: to abuse one's authority.
POWER, WHILE AUTHORITY WITHOUT POWER IS POINTLESS
POINTLESS is it has no use or makes no sense, worthless, lacking in usefulness or value

THE POWER OF THE WORD OF GOD

THE WORD OF GOD IS AN ACCURATE PRESENTATION OF THE TRUTH OF GOD, SERVES TO PURIFY AND GUIDE
IN THE EPISTLE TO THE HEBREWS, THE POWER OF THE WORD OF GOD IS DESCRIBED " FOR THE WORD OF GOD IS LIVING AND ACTIVE. SHARPER THAN ANY DOUBLE - EDGED SWORD, IT PENETRATES EVEN DIVIDING SOUL AND SPIRIT, JOINTS AND MARROW, IT JUDGES THE THOUGHTS AND ATTITUDES OF THE HEART" (Hebrews 4:12)

AUTHORITY- THE BLESSINGS

4. POWER OF THE HOLY SPIRIT
MOMENT BY MOMENT
DAY BY DAY

LIVING BY THE SPIRIT IS DEPENDING MOMENT BY MOMENT ON THE POWER OF THE SPIRIT TO OVERCOME OUR OWN INADEQUACY.

ACCORDINGLY, THE LIFE OF VICTORY, SUCCESS AND PROSPERITY IS A LIFE OF FAITH AS WE LIVE DAY BY DAY, RELYING ON THE HOLY SPIRIT TO GIVE US POWER TO SERVE THE LORD EFFECTIVELY.

RELY UPON THE POWER OF THE HOLY SPIRIT TO ACHIEVE WHAT YOU SHOULD BY WAY OF OBEDIENCE AND COMMITMENT TO GOD.

HONORING GOD, REST IN THE POWER OF THE HOLY SPIRIT, THE SPIRIT OF GOD CAN SUPPORT YOU AND CARRY YOU MOMENT BY MOMENT IN YOUR SERVICE AND TESTIMONY FOR THE LORD.

AUTHORITY- THE BLESSINGS

5. AUTHORITY IS

AUTHORITY IS THE RIGHT TO DO IT

Authority. The power or right to give commands, enforce obedience, take action, or make final decisions; jurisdiction. The position of one having such power: a person in authority.

Noun
1. The power or right to give orders, make decisions, and enforce obedience. "He had absolute authority over his subordinates" synonyms: power, jurisdiction, command, control, charge, dominance, rule, sovereignty, supremacy; more
2. A person or organization having power or control in a particular, typically political or administrative, sphere "the health authority" synonyms: officials, officialdom; more.

THE AUTHORITY OF THE BEHAVIOR

The doctrine of the authority of the believer is used in characteristic circles to claim divine power to perform miracles, get rich, stay healthy, bind Satan, speak a new reality into existence, or whatever else the believer wants to happen. Before we start enumerating the things that fall under the authority of the believer, we must acknowledge that, first and foremost, the believer is under authority. God is the authority. Believers should point to God's authority. The believer's life is one total dependence on God, as modeled by the son of man.

AUTHORITY- THE BLESSINGS

6. CHRIST, GRACE - GIVEN AUTHORITY

JESUS CHRIST

Christ has given every follower his power and authority to defeat Satan and all evil spirits. His power is greater than the power of the enemy. When there is a head- on conflict between the power of the enemy and the power of God, the power of the enemy will lose every time.

It is not that we have God - given authority over Satan; rather it is that Christ in us does. As John wrote "Greater is he that is in you than he that is in the world". (1 John 4:4)

7. TAKING AUTHORITY

Take authority and regain dominion and control

Do not allow circumstances or words and actions of others, adversaries to stop you from releasing your faith to speaking what God has said in his word and believe that your word will come to pass.

Speaking in faith you will see the promised manifestation of God's power in your life.

You have the spiritual authority to rise above their actions and words.

Satan recognizes and fears the power of God.

AUTHORITY- THE BLESSINGS

8. SPEAKING AUTHORITY
We have been given Authority
"In the name of Jesus"

You and I represent Jesus! We can walk in authority in his name because we are his representatives.

The name of Jesus is a weapon to use to enforce Satan's defeat. Jesus' name can do anything he can do. And he is totally unlimited. Jesus defeated Satan, Satan wants to keep you confused, fearful, sick, lacking and hurt emotionally so you won't know and believe the power and authority you have!

He wants you to see your circumstances and not trust the word of God. Keep you from reading the bible and learn that there are things promised to you that you were unaware you can have here on this earth.

The power behind the name of Jesus is the power of almighty God. When we speak the name of Jesus the power that comes out of your mouth is the power of almighty God himself! (Philippians 2: 9-10).

9. SPEAKING WITH AUTHORITY

AS GOD HIMSELF WAS SPEAKING IT

The power is in the word of God. The power and authority you have been given to speak, exercise, make use and release the word of God with faith and authority over your circumstances, use the name of Jesus, you have been given to take back what the devil has stolen from you!

AUTHORITY- THE BLESSINGS

10. LIVE AND WALK IN THIS POWER AND AUTHORITY
The world we live in has two realms
The physical Realm
The Spiritual Realm

To be effective in the world realm, we must do two things.
1. Walk with God in a personal relationship and have nothing before him in our heart.
2. Walk in the dominion that God has given us in the world realm.

11. The Physical Realm-
The world is represented by violence, cruelty, greed, frustration, anger, disappointment, destruction and competition.

12. The Spiritual Realm-
It is characterized by love, compassion, acceptance, tolerance, humility, growth and cooperation. Concluding "they could not be more different" The magnitude of the difference results from our personal stance between the two and the collective attitude of all people: The mankind if need not to be so great. The physical world will never be the spiritual world, but the two worlds can be more congruent.

13. Spiritual Realm, Characteristics in the Physical Realm-
The difference between the two realms, the immutable characteristics are things we can do nothing about. They have been established in this way to provide the physical world we are experiencing. We have no control over them- they're complete opposites.

AUTHORITY - THE BLESSING

Spiritual Realm Characteristics in the Physical Realm
IMMUTABLE CHARACTERISTICS

14. Immutable Characteristics-
    1. The Physical Realm
        a. Beginning and ending
        b. Time
        c. Space
        d. Entropy, decay, death, cold, inanimate, dust to dust, cause and effect
        e. Separation
    2. Spiritual Realm
        a. No beginning, No ending
        b. Timeless
        c. Spacelessness
        d. Eternal life
        e. Warmth, life and organic
        f. Is and Oneness

We must learn how to live in this spiritual realm in a way that affects the physical realm. Instead of the spiritual realm only affecting me, I need to be living in a way that affects the spiritual realm, which in turn affects the physical realm.

AUTHORITY- THE BLESSINGS
Spiritual Realm Characteristics in the Physical Realm
THE CONSENSUS CHARACTERISTICS

15. The Consensus Characteristics- that result from consensus of human thoughts, sentiments and behavior. They are under our control as individuals and as a species.

THE PHYSICAL REALM:	THE SPIRITUAL REALM:
Violence	Non- violence
Hate	Love
Self- centeredness	Other- centeredness
Unhappiness	Joy
Separation	Bring together
Anger	Compassion
Impatience	Patient
Harshness	Gentleness
Unethical behavior	Ethical behavior
Strife, war	Peace
Dishonesty	Honesty
Deceit	Truth
Cruelty	Comforting
Manipulation	Aid
Arrogance	Humility
Evil	Goodness
Rejection, separation	Acceptance
Intolerance	Tolerance

PRESENT, The quantity of the negative characteristics present in the physical world is very large and the quantity of the positive or spiritual characteristics is very small. However, that higher proportion of negative characteristics is a result of choice we are making as a species, not the structure established for the physical realm. We have more of the negative because of a consensus we have about having more of it.

AUTHORITY- THE BLESSINGS

THE PHYSICAL REALM

PHYSICAL- phys - i - cal

16. Physical Is, definition

Adjective
1. Relating to the body as opposed to the mind "a whole range of physical and mental challenges"
   synonyms: bodily, corporeal, corporal, somatic; more
2. Relating to things perceived through the senses as opposed to the mind; tangible or concrete. "Pleasant physical environments"
   synonyms: material, concrete, tangible, palpable, solid, substantial, real, actual, visible "the physical universe"

Noun
1. A medical examination to determine a person's bodily fitness.

REALM- [relm]
17. Realm Is, definition

Noun
A royal domain; Kingdom:
1. The realm of England
2. "The region, sphere, or domain within which anything occurs, prevails, or dominates: the realm of dreams.
3. The special province or field of something or someone: the realm of physics; facts within the realm of political scientists"

AUTHORITY- THE BLESSINGS

Spiritual Realm Characteristics in the Physical Realm

The Spiritual Realm

18. Spiritual Is, definition

Adjective
1. Relating to the spirit or soul and not to physical nature of matter; intangible
2. Of, relating to, or characteristics of sacred things, the church, religion, etc.
3. Standing in a relationship based on communication between the souls or minds of the person involved. "A special father"
4. Having a mind or emotions of a high and delicately refined quality.

Noun
1. Negro spiritual- a type of religious songs originating among black slaves in american south.
2. The sphere of religious, spiritual, or ecclesiastical matters, or such matters in themselves
3. The. the realm of the spirits
    a. Spiritually- adjective
    b. Spiritualness- noun

B.
AUTHORITY- THE DEMONSTRATIONS
AUTHORITY- DEMONSTRATIONS
Into your life
Into other people lives
"IN THE NAME OF JESUS"
Section one
TAKING AUTHORITY

Taking Authority- Releasing Power, Strength and Authority
1. Ministering, healing and serving into my life
2. I am taking authority, releasing my power to regain my eye sight
3. [self] make use of your authority, exercise it.

IN THE NAME OF JESUS,
I'm a physical man/woman,
A man/woman of God,
I have been given Authority
By the almighty God,
And right here, right now,
I take Authority,
I speak to my eye sight,
EYES,
You see perfectly,
I command it,
Right now,
IN THE NAME OF JESUS
as a man/woman,
authorized by God,
my vision, see clearly and perfect,
eyes be healed,
Right now,
IN THE NAME OF JESUS.

AUTHORITY- THE DEMONSTRATIONS

THE DEMONSTRATIONS- TAKING AUTHORITY

Releasing power, strength and authority
1. Ministering, healing and serving into other people lives
2. Taking authority, regaining eyesight and clear vision in another person's life.
3. [believer's] speak and release your power.

Heavenly Father,
IN THE NAME OF JESUS,
I command (   ),
eyesight to be restored,
vision - extremely clear,
oh my God,
noticeable do it,
Right now,
not tomorrow,
I command (   ),
eyes to be completely healed,
Right now,
eyes- vision,
be healed,
IN THE NAME OF JESUS.

AUTHORITY- THE DEMONSTRATION

THE DEMONSTRATION- TAKING AUTHORITY

Releasing power, strength and authority
1. Ministering, healing and serving into my life.
2. I am taking authority, releasing my power to strengthen and regain my hearing.
3. [self] make use of your authority, exercise it.

IN THE NAME OF JESUS,
I'm a physical man/woman,
a man/woman of God,
I have been given
Authority,
by the almighty God,
and right here,
Right now,
I take authority,
I speak authority,
I speak to my ears,
EARS TO HEAR,
EARS,
ears you hear perfectly,
I command it now,

IN THE NAME OF JESUS.
as a man/woman,
authorized by God,
my hearing- hear clearly,
EAR GATES,
BE HEALED,
Right now,
IN THE NAME OF JESUS.

AUTHORITY- THE DEMONSTRATIONS

THE DEMONSTRATIONS- TAKING AUTHORITY

Releasing power, strength and authority
1. Ministering, healing and serving into my life.
2. I am taking authority, releasing my power to strengthen and regain my hearing.
3. [believer's] speak and release your power.

Heavenly Father,
IN THE NAME OF JESUS,
I command (   ),
ear gates to be open,
regaining and restoring (   ),
hEARING TO THE FULLEST,
extremely clear,
oh my God,
noticeable do it,
Right now,
not tomorrow,
I command (   ),
ears to be totally healed,
Right now,
EARS- ears gates,
Hearing,
BE HEALED,
IN THE NAME OF JESUS,
as a man/woman,
authorized by God,
(   ) hearing- hear clearly,
EAR GATES,
BE HEALED,
RIGHT NOW,
IN THE NAME OF JESUS.

AUTHORITY- THE DEMONSTRATIONS

THE DEMONSTRATIONS
Into your life
Into other people lives
Section Two
Authority over pain in the body

Releasing authority to relieve pain forever
1. Ministering, healing and serving into my life.
2. Releasing my authority to relieve pain in my body.
3. [self] exercising your authority.

IN THE NAME OF JESUS,
I have authority,
given to me by God,
with this power,
that I have a right
to use it,
Therefore,
IN THE NAME OF JESUS,
I command this pain,
all pains in my body,
to leave my body,
Right now,
I'm not asking, arguing or begging,
I am taking authority
over the pain in my body,
I command this pain,
to cease all operations,
Right now
Pain- stop and go,
Body be pain free,
Body be healed,
IN THE NAME OF JESUS.

AUTHORITY- THE DEMONSTRATIONS

THE DEMONSTRATIONS- AUTHORITY OVER PAIN IN THE BODY

Releasing authority to relieve pain forever.
1. Ministering, healing and serving into your life.
2. Releasing your authority to relieve pain in your body.
3. [believer's] speak and release your power and authority.

IN THE NAME OF JESUS,
I, (   ) have authority
given to me by God,
with this power,
that I have a right
to use it,
Therefore,
IN THE NAME OF JESUS,
I command this pain,
(   ) in my body
to leave my body,
Right now,
I'm not asking, arguing or begging,
I am taking authority
over the pain in my body.
I command this (   )
to cease all operations,
Right now,
(   )- stop and go,
body be pain- free.
body be healed.
IN THE NAME OF JESUS.

AUTHORITY- THE DEMONSTRATIONS

THE DEMONSTRATIONS- AUTHORITY OVER THE PAIN IN MY BODY

Releasing authority to relieve pain forever.
1. Ministering, healing and serving other people's lives.
2. Releasing my authority, relieving pain from other people's bodies.
3. [believer's] make use of your authority.

By Authority, God- given Authority invested in me.
Father,
I command the pain
In (_his/her name_) body,
to be completely healed,
100% pain free,
Right now,
IN THE NAME OF JESUS,
I stretch forth my hands
to you Father,
for healing in
(_his/her name_) body,
body be healed,
Right now,
IN THE NAME OF JESUS.

IN THE NAME OF JESUS,
Father, I stretch forth my hands to you God,
for healing in (_names of family/friends, more_) bodies,
by the Authority, God- given Authority
placed on my Bornagain Spirit.
I command (_names of family/friends, more_)
to be completely healed 100% pain free,
Right now, body be healed,
Right now,
IN THE NAME OF JESUS.

AUTHORITY- THE DEMONSTRATIONS

THE DEMONSTRATIONS,
Into your life.
Into other people's lives.

Section Three
Authority over skin disease, the healing of the skin.

Releasing authority to heal the skin,
1. Ministering, healing and serving into my life.
2. Releasing authority to heal the skin
3. [self] exercising authority for healing.

IN THE NAME OF JESUS,
I release my authority
to heal the skin,
IN THE NAME OF JESUS
I speak to my skin,
I speak to my body,
And I speak
to the skin disease,
leave me now,
get off my skin,
I am healed,
Right now,
IN THE NAME OF JESUS.

AUTHORITY- THE DEMONSTRATIONS

THE DEMONSTRATIONS- AUTHORITY OVER SKIN DISEASE, THE HEALING OF THE SKIN.

Releasing authority to heal the skin,
1. Ministering, healing and serving other people's lives.
2. Releasing authority for the healing of the skin.
3. [believer's] exercising authority for healing into other people's lives.

IN THE NAME OF JESUS,
I release my authority
to heal other people,
IN THE NAME OF JESUS,
I speak to the skin
on (his/her name) body,
and I speak
to the skin disease on
(his/her name) body,
to leave (his/her name) body
Right now,
get off (his/her name) skin,
leave (his/her name) body,
I call you healed,
Right now,
IN THE NAME OF JESUS.

AUTHORITY- THE DEMONSTRATIONS

THE DEMONSTRATIONS- AUTHORITY OVER SKIN DISEASE, THE HEALING OF THE SKIN.

Releasing authority to heal the skin,
1. Ministering, healing and serving into my life, your life.
2. Releasing authority for the healing of your skin.
3. [self] exercising authority for healing.

FATHER,
IN THE NAME OF JESUS,
I stretch forth my hands,
I release my authority,
Right now,
I command,
my body and skin disease,
to go- leave me now,
IN THE NAME OF JESUS.
skin clear up,
skin be disease free,
Right now,
IN THE NAME OF JESUS.

AUTHORITY- THE DEMONSTRATIONS

THE DEMONSTRATIONS- AUTHORITY OVER SKIN DISEASE, THE HEALING OF THE SKIN.

Releasing authority for the healing of the skin,
1. Ministering, healing and serving other people's lives.
2. Releasing authority for the healing of the skin.
3. [believer's] exercising authority for healing into other people's lives.

FATHER,
IN THE NAME OF JESUS,
I stretch forth my hands,
I place my hands on (his/her name) body,
I release my authority,
Right now,
and I command,
(his/her name) body and skin disease,
To go and leave (his/her name) body,
IN THE NAME OF JESUS,
skin clear up,
be disease free,
be healed,
Right now,
IN THE NAME OF JESUS.

AUTHORITY- THE DEMONSTRATIONS

THE DEMONSTRATIONS,
Into your life.
Into other people's lives.

Section Four
Authority over sickness, disease and inflammation

Releasing authority and power,
1. Ministering, healing and serving into your life.
2. Releasing my authority to relieve inflammation.
3. [self] exercising authority for healing.

IN THE NAME OF JESUS,
I have been given authority
by God almighty, The almighty God.
I have the authority
and the right,
to command sickness, disease
and inflammation.
In my body to be gone.
IN THE NAME OF JESUS,
Therefore,
Inflammation in my knees, body
and the cellular parts
of my body,
I command you to go,
Right now,
I am healed.
IN THE NAME OF JESUS.

AUTHORITY- THE DEMONSTRATIONS

THE DEMONSTRATIONS- AUTHORITY OVER SICKNESS, DISEASE AND INFLAMMATION.

Releasing authority and power,
1. Ministering, healing and serving into your life.
2. Releasing your authority relieves inflammation.
3. [believer's] speak and release authority for healing.

IN THE NAME OF JESUS,
I, (your name), have been given authority,
by the almighty God.
I, (your name), have the authority,
and the right.
I, (your name) command,
sickness, disease and inflammation,
In my body,
to be gone.IN THE NAME OF JESUS,
Therefore,
Inflammation in my knees,
body and the cellular
parts of my body,
I command you to go,
Right now,
I am healed.
IN THE NAME OF JESUS.

AUTHORITY- THE DEMONSTRATIONS

THE DEMONSTRATIONS- AUTHORITY OVER SICKNESS, DISEASE AND INFLAMMATION.

Releasing authority and power.
1. Ministering, healing and serving other people's lives.
2. Releasing your authority for healing in other people's lives.
3. [believer's] speak and release authority for healing into other people's lives.

NOW FATHER,
I stretch forth my hands to you.
I command sickness,
disease and inflammation
In (_____) body
To be gone.
sickness and disease- to be gone,
for every pain- to be gone,
Inflammation- to be gone,
knees be healed,
Right now,
IN THE NAME OF JESUS,
LORD,
I GIVE YOU PRAISE
FOR THAT,
RIGHT NOW
IN THE NAME OF JESUS.

AUTHORITY- THE DEMONSTRATIONS

THE DEMONSTRATIONS,
Into your life.
Into other people's lives.

Section Five
Authority over pains in the human body and joints.

Releasing authority to remove pain in the joints.
1. Ministering, healing and serving into my life.
2. Releasing my authority to relieve the pain in my joints
3. [self] releasing my authority, relieving pain in my joints.

IN THE NAME OF JESUS,
I have been given authority,
by the almighty God.
I have the authority
and the right to use it.
I command,
for every pain in my ligaments,
my knees, hands, feet, ankles,
hips, elbows and shoulders,
to be gone.
Right now,
IN THE NAME OF JESUS,
Therefore,
pain in my ligaments,
pain in my body,
I command you to go.
joint be pain free,
ligaments be healed,
Right now,
IN THE NAME OF JESUS.

AUTHORITY- THE DEMONSTRATIONS

THE DEMONSTRATIONS- AUTHORITY OVER PAINS IN THE HUMAN BODY AND JOINTS.

Releasing authority to remove pain in the joints,
1. Ministering, healing and serving into your life.
2. Releasing your authority removes the pain in your joints.
3. [believer's] speak and release your authority for healing.

IN THE NAME OF JESUS,
I, (_____), have been given authority,
by the almighty God.
I, (_____), have the authority
and the right to use it.
I, (_____), command
for every pain in my ligaments,
my knees, hands, feet, ankles,
hips, elbows and shoulders,
to be gone.
Right now,
IN THE NAME OF JESUS,
Therefore,
pain in my ligament,
pain in my body,
I command you to go.
Ligaments be healed,
body be healed,
Right now,
IN THE NAME OF JESUS.

AUTHORITY- THE DEMONSTRATIONS

THE DEMONSTRATIONS- AUTHORITY OVER PAINS IN THE HUMAN BODY AND JOINTS.

Releasing authority to remove pains in the joints,
1. Ministering, healing and serving into other people's lives.
2. Releasing authority removes joint pains in other people's lives.
3. [believer's] speak and release authority for healing into other people's lives.

NOW FATHER,
I stretch forth my hands to you.
I command the ligaments
In the human body of
(his/her name), for every pain,
to be gone,
Right now,
In (his/her name), knees, hands, feet,
ankles, hips, elbows and shoulders,
To be pain free.
Right now,
IN THE NAME OF JESUS,
LORD,
I GIVE YOU PRAISE
FOR THAT,
RIGHT NOW,
IN THE NAME OF JESUS.

AUTHORITY- THE DEMONSTRATIONS

THE DEMONSTRATIONS,
Into your life.
Into other people's lives.

Section Six
Authority over Mind and Thoughts
The healing of depression, stress and suicidal thoughts.

Releasing your authority for healing,
1. Ministering, healing and serving into my life.
2. Releasing authority for healing of depression.
3. [self] exercising my authority for healing from depression.

IN THE NAME OF JESUS,
I release my authority
to heal myself from depression,
all worries, cares and fears,
I speak to my mind and thoughts
and
I speak to my depression, stress
and suicidal thoughts.
I command,
depression, stress, and or suicidal thoughts,
to leave my mind.
get out of my thoughts,
Right now,
IN THE NAME OF JESUS,
I am free of worries, cares and fears,
depression, stress and or suicidal thoughts.
be gone,
I AM HEALED,
RIGHT NOW,
IN THE NAME OF JESUS.

AUTHORITY- THE DEMONSTRATIONS

THE DEMONSTRATIONS- AUTHORITY OVER MIND AND THOUGHTS.

The healing of depression, stress and suicidal thoughts.

Releasing authority for healing,
1. Ministering, healing and serving into your life.
2. Releasing authority for healing of depression.
3. [self]exercising your authority for healing from depression.

IN THE NAME OF JESUS,
I, (his/her name), release my authority
to heal myself from depression
worries, cares and fears.
I, (his/her name), speak to my mind and thoughts
and
I, (his/her name), speak to my depression,
stress and or suicidal thoughts.
I, (his/her name), command depression,
stress and or suicidal thoughts,
to leave my mind.
get out of my thoughts,
Right now,
IN THE NAME OF JESUS,
I am free of worries,cares and fears,
depression, stress and or suicidal thoughts.
be gone,
I AM HEALED,
 RIGHT NOW,
IN THE NAME OF JESUS.

AUTHORITY- THE DEMONSTRATIONS

THE DEMONSTRATIONS- AUTHORITY OVER MIND AND THOUGHTS.

The healing of depression, stress and suicidal thoughts.

Releasing authority for healing,
1. Ministering, healing and serving into your life.
2. Releasing authority for healing of depression.
3. [self] exercising your authority for healing from depression.

FATHER,
IN THE NAME OF JESUS,
I raise my hands to you God,
I release my authority,
Right now,
ceasing all temptations
on my mind and thoughts,
I command,
the depression, stress and or
suicidal thoughts,
In my mind - to go,
get out of my thoughts,
Right now,
IN THE NAME OF JESUS,
My mind and thoughts,
free from worries, cares and fears,
free from depression, stress and or
suicidal thoughts,
I AM HEALED,
Right now,
IN THE NAME OF JESUS.

AUTHORITY- THE DEMONSTRATIONS

THE DEMONSTRATIONS- AUTHORITY OVER MIND AND THOUGHTS

The healing of depression, stress and suicidal thoughts.

Releasing authority for healing,
1. Ministering, healing and serving into other people's lives.
2. Releasing authority for healing from depression.
3. [believer's] speak and release authority for healing from depression into other people's lives.

FATHER,
IN THE NAME OF JESUS,
I raise my hands to you God,
I release my authority,
RIGHT NOW,
IN THE NAME OF JESUS,
To cease all temptations
on (_his/her name_), mind and thoughts,
I command,
The depression, stress and or
suicidal thoughts
In (_his/her name_), mind- to go,
get out of (_his/her name_), thoughts
RIGHT NOW,
(_his/her name_), mind and thoughts,
be free of worries, cares and fears,
all depression, stress and or
suicidal thoughts,
be gone,
I call you healed,
Right now,
IN THE NAME OF JESUS.

AUTHORITY- THE DEMONSTRATIONS

THE DEMONSTRATIONS,
Into your life.
Into other people's lives.
Section Seven
Authority over the failure of organs in the human body.

Releasing authority to restore organ functions in the body.
1. Ministering, healing and serving into my life.
2. Exercising and releasing my authority.
3. [self] making use of my authority for healing.

IN THE NAME OF JESUS,
by the almighty God,
I have been given authority,
I have the authority
and the right to use it.
IN THE NAME OF JESUS.
I command, the organ failure in my body,
to be gone.
In my heart, lungs, kidneys, liver,
pancreas and wherever failure
lies in my body.
failure cease,
restore 100% perfect,
Right now,
IN THE NAME OF JESUS.
Therefore,
failure in my body,
organ(s) in my human body.
I command my organ(s)
to be fully restored,
I am healed
IN THE NAME OF JESUS.

AUTHORITY- THE DEMONSTRATIONS

THE DEMONSTRATIONS- AUTHORITY OVER THE FAILURE OF ORGANS IN THE HUMAN BODY.

Releasing authority to restore organ functions in the body.
1. Ministering, healing and serving into my life.
2. Exercising and releasing your authority.
3. [self] making use of your authority for healing.

IN THE NAME OF JESUS,
I, (_____), have authority
given to me by God
and the right to use it.
I, (_____), command
the organ(s) failure in my body,
to be gone - now,
In my heart, lungs, kidneys, liver,
pancreas and or wherever
failure lies in my body.
restore 100% perfect,
Right now,
IN THE NAME OF JESUS.
Therefore,
Failure in my body,
organ(s) in my human body,
I command you
to be fully restored,
I am healed,
IN THE NAME OF JESUS.

AUTHORITY- THE DEMONSTRATIONS

THE DEMONSTRATIONS- AUTHORITY OVER THE FAILURE OF ORGANS IN THE HUMAN BODY.

Releasing authority to restore organ functions in the body.
1. Ministering, healing and serving into other people's lives.
2. Exercising and releasing my authority.
3. [believer's] speak and release authority into other people's lives.

HEAVENLY FATHER,
I stretch forth my hands to you,
IN THE NAME OF JESUS.
I command the organ(s) failure(s)
In, (   ), body
to be gone,
Right now,
IN THE NAME OF JESUS,
In, (   ), heart, lungs, kidneys,
liver, pancreas and wherever failure may lie
In, (   ), body,
failure be gone,
organ(s) be healed,
Right now,
IN THE NAME OF JESUS.
LORD, I GIVE YOU
PRAISE FOR THAT
RIGHT NOW
IN THE NAME OF JESUS.

AUTHORITY- THE DEMONSTRATIONS

THE DEMONSTRATIONS- AUTHORITY OVER THE FAILURE OF ORGANS IN THE HUMAN BODY.

Releasing authority restoring organ functions in the human body.
1. Ministering, healing and serving into other people's lives.
2. Exercising and releasing your authority.
3. [believer's] speaking and releasing authority for healing into other people's lives.

HEAVENLY FATHER,
I stretch forth my hands to you
IN THE NAME OF JESUS,
I command the organ(s) failure
In, (his/her name), body
To be gone,
Right now,
IN THE NAME OF JESUS,
In, (his/her name), (name of organ ex. Kidney's),
and any other organ(s) failure or complications
In, (his/her name), body
failure be gone,
restored 100% perfect,
(name of organ(s) _____)(_____),
be healed,
Right now,
IN THE NAME OF JESUS,
LORD,
I GIVE YOU PRAISE
FOR THAT,
RIGHT NOW,
IN THE NAME OF JESUS.

AUTHORITY - THE DEMONSTRATIONS

THE DEMONSTRATIONS,
Into your life.
Into other people's lives.

Section Eight
Authority over lack and poverty.

Releasing authority to remove lack and poverty,
1. Ministering, healing and serving into your life.
2. Exercising and releasing my authority.
3. [self] exercising my authority to end lack and poverty.

IN THE NAME OF JESUS,
I have authority
given to me by God,
with this power
that I have the right
to use it, therefore,
IN THE NAME OF JESUS,
I command the lack in my life,
poverty in my life
to leave my life,
Right now,
lack of shelter, clothing, food,
education, health care, employment
and or any other thing I may lack
In my life,
to be gone,
I command the lack and poverty
In my life
to cease fight now,
IN THE NAME OF JESUS.

AUTHORITY- THE DEMONSTRATIONS

THE DEMONSTRATIONS- AUTHORITY OVER LACK AND POVERTY.

Releasing authority to remove lack and poverty,
1. Ministering, healing and serving into your life.
2. Exercising and releasing your authority.
3. [self] making use of your authority to end lack and poverty in your life.

IN THE NAME OF JESUS,
I, (   ), release my authority
to be healed
from lack and poverty.
Right now,
be free of lack and poverty.
IN THE NAME OF JESUS.
I, (   ), command lack and poverty
In my life to forever leave me,
Right now,
I, (   ), command all my needs,
wants and desires of my heart
pertaining to life and godliness
into my life.
my life to overflow in abundance,
Right now,
IN THE NAME OF JESUS.
LORD,
I GIVE YOU PRAISE
FOR ABUNDANCE IN MY LIFE,
RIGHT NOW,
IN THE NAME OF JESUS.

AUTHORITY- THE DEMONSTRATIONS

THE DEMONSTRATIONS- AUTHORITY OVER LACK AND POVERTY.

Releasing authority to remove lack and poverty.
1. Ministering, healing and serving into my life.
2. Exercising and releasing my authority.
3. [self] exercising my authority to end lack and poverty in my life.

IN THE NAME OF JESUS,
I release my authority
to be healed
from lack and poverty in my life.
Right now,
be free of lack and poverty.
IN THE NAME OF JESUS,
I command lack and poverty in my life
to forever leave me.
Right now,
I command all my needs, wants and
desires of my heart pertaining to life
and godliness into my life.
My life to overflow in abundance,
Right now,
IN THE NAME OF JESUS.
LORD,
I GIVE PRAISE FOR
ABUNDANCE IN MY LIFE,
RIGHT NOW,
IN THE NAME OF JESUS.

AUTHORITY- THE DEMONSTRATIONS

THE DEMONSTRATIONS- AUTHORITY OVER LACK AND POVERTY.

Releasing authority to remove lack and poverty,
1. Ministering, healing and serving into your life.
2. Exercising and releasing your authority.
3. [self] making use of your authority to end lack and poverty in your life.

IN THE NAME OF JESUS,
I, (your name), have authority
given to me by God,
with this power that
I have the right to use it.
Therefore,
IN THE NAME OF JESUS,
I, (your name), command the lack in my life,
The poverty in my life
to leave my life,
Right now,
The lack of shelter, clothing, food, education,
healthcare, employment and or any other
things I may lack in my life,
To be gone.
IN THE NAME OF JESUS.
I, (your name), command ,
lack and poverty in my life to cease,
Right now,
IN THE NAME OF JESUS.

AUTHORITY- THE DEMONSTRATIONS

THE DEMONSTRATIONS- AUTHORITY OVER LACK AND POVERTY.

Releasing authority to remove lack and poverty,
1. Ministering, healing and serving into other people's lives.
2. Exercising and releasing your authority.
3. [believer's] speak and release your authority to remove lack and poverty from other people's lives.

By the authority
invested in me,
FATHER,
I command, (_his/her name_), to be
completely healed,
Completely from lack and poverty
In, (_his/her name_), life
Right now,
IN JESUS NAME,
I stretch forth my hands
to you FATHER,
For the lack of shelter, clothing, food,
education, healthcare, employment,
and or any other things that (_his/her name_),
may lack in, (_his/her name_), life to cease,
Right now,
IN THE NAME OF JESUS.

AUTHORITY- THE DEMONSTRATIONS

THE DEMONSTRATIONS- AUTHORITY OVER LACK AND POVERTY.

Releasing authority to remove lack and poverty,
1. Ministering, healing and serving into other people's lives.
2. Exercising and releasing your authority.
3. [believer's] speak and release your authority to remove lack and poverty from other people's lives.

FATHER,
IN THE NAME OF JESUS,
I stretch forth my hands to you,
I place my hands on
(_____), life.
I release my authority,
Right now,
IN THE NAME OF JESUS.
and I command
the lack and poverty in
(_____),
life to end,
leave (_____), life
Right now,
IN THE NAME OF JESUS.
lack of shelter, clothing, food, education,
healthcare, employment and or
any other lack in, (_____), life
to be gone,
Right now,
IN THE NAME OF JESUS.

AUTHORITY- THE DEMONSTRATIONS

THE DEMONSTRATIONS- AUTHORITY OVER LACK AND POVERTY.

Releasing authority to remove lack and poverty.
1. Ministering, healing and serving into other people's lives.
2. Exercising and releasing your authority.
3. [believer's] speak and release your authority to remove lack and poverty from other people's lives.

FATHER,
IN THE NAME OF JESUS,
I raise my hands to you,
I release my authority,
Right now,
IN THE NAME OF JESUS,
ceasing the lack of poverty
in, (_____),life,
I command the lack and poverty
in, (_____), life to end.
Right now,
IN THE NAME OF JESUS.
I command, (_____), needs, wants
and desires of, (_____), heart pertaining
to life and godliness into, (_____), life
to overflow in abundance.
IN THE NAME OF JESUS,
LORD, I GIVE YOU PRAISE
FOR THE ABUNDANCE
IN, (_____), life
Right now
IN THE NAME OF JESUS.

AUTHORITY- THE DEMONSTRATIONS

THE DEMONSTRATIONS- AUTHORITY OVER LACK AND POVERTY.

Releasing authority to remove lack and poverty,
1. Ministering, healing and serving into other people's lives.
2. Exercising and releasing your authority.
3. [believer's] speak and release your authority to remove lack and poverty from other people's lives.

HEAVENLY FATHER,
I stretch forth my hands to you,
I place my hands
on (his/her name), life
I release my authority,
Right now
IN THE NAME OF JESUS
and I command
the lack and poverty
In, (his/her name), life to end,
In, (his/her name), life
Right now
IN THE NAME OF JESUS,
I command, (his/her name), needs, wants,
and the desires of, (his/her name), heart
pertaining to life and godliness into, (his/her name),
life overflows in abundance.
IN THE NAME OF JESUS,
LORD,
I GIVE YOU PRAISE
FOR THE ABUNDANCE
IN, (his/her name), life
Right now,
IN THE NAME OF JESUS.

AUTHORITY - THE DEMONSTRATIONS

THE DEMONSTRATIONS,
Into your life.
Into other people's lives.

Section Nine
Authority over demons and evil spirits in the human body.

Releasing authority to cast out demons and evil spirits.
1. Ministering, healing and serving into my life.
2. Releasing authority to cast out demons and evil spirits that are in the human body.
3. [self] taking and releasing authority commanding satan and all evil out of my life.

I HAVE AUTHORITY,
IN JESUS NAME
Given to me by God,
with this power,
I command Satan, demon spirits,
and evil spirits to cease.
All maneuvers, operations
and temptations in my life.
Right now,
IN THE NAME OF JESUS.

No evils will enter and or rent
space in my human body.
Get out of my body, mind and thoughts,
Right now,
IN THE NAME OF JESUS.

I command satan,
all evils and his servants
to cease all maneuvers, operations and temptations,
Right now.
IN THE NAME OF JESUS.

I am taking authority
to cease all temptations
to rent space in my body,
Right now.

IN THE NAME ABOVE ALL NAMES.

IN THE NAME OF JESUS.

AUTHORITY- THE DEMONSTRATIONS

THE DEMONSTRATIONS- AUTHORITY OVER DEMONS AND EVIL SPIRITS IN THE HUMAN BODY.

Releasing authority to cast out demons and evil spirits.
1. Ministering, healing and serving into other people's lives.
2. Releasing your authority to cast out demons and evil spirits that's controlling the minds and thoughts in other people's lives.
3. [believer's] taking and releasing authority, commanding satan and all evils out of other people's lives.

I HAVE AUTHORITY,
IN JESUS NAME,
Given to me by God,
with this power,
I command satan,
demons and evil spirits
to leave, (_____), human body.
Get out of, (_____), mind and thoughts,
Right now,
IN THE NAME OF JESUS.
I command satan
and all evils to cease
all maneuvers, operations and temptations
on, (_____), life.
Leave- Go- Now- Immediately
IN THE NAME OF JESUS.

I AM TAKING AUTHORITY,
I AM RELEASING MY AUTHORITY,
IN THE NAME OF JESUS.
Therefore,
Satan and all evils,
No more renting space
and sinful acts in, (_his/her name_), body.
I AM EVICTING YOU SATAN
AND ALL EVILS
FROM, (_his/her name_), HUMAN BODY
RIGHT NOW.

IN THE NAME ABOVE ALL NAMES,

IN THE NAME OF JESUS.

AUTHORITY- THE DEMONSTRATIONS

THE DEMONSTRATIONS,
Into your life.
Into other people's lives.
Section Ten
Authority over cancer in the human body.

Releasing authority to remove cancer in the human body.
1. Ministering, healing and serving into my life.
2. Releasing my authority to remove cancer from my body.
3. [self] Exercising my authority for healing in my body.

IN THE NAME OF JESUS,
I have authority
given to me by God
with this power that
I have a right to use it.
Therefore,
IN THE NAME OF JESUS,
I command this cancer to be gone.
IN THE NAME OF JESUS,
Cancer, in my breast, brains,
colon, prostate, bones and in any
part of my human body
to leave my body, right now.
IN THE NAME OF JESUS.
I'm not asking, I'm taking authority.
I command this cancer to cease
all operations in my human body,
Right now,
cancer - stop- and go, right now.
IN THE NAME OF JESUS.

AUTHORITY- THE DEMONSTRATIONS

THE DEMONSTRATIONS- AUTHORITY OVER CANCER IN THE HUMAN BODY.

Releasing authority to remove cancer in the human body.
1. Ministering, healing and serving into your life'
2. Releasing your authority to remove cancer out of your body.
3. [self] Exercising your authority for healing in your body.

IN THE NAME OF JESUS,
I, (_your name_), have authority
given to me by God
with this power that
I have the right to use it.
Therefore,
IN THE NAME OF JESUS,
I, (_your name_), command this cancer
in, (_your name_), and or any other
part in my human body
to leave my body,
Right now,
IN THE NAME OF JESUS.
I'm not asking,
I'm taking authority,
I, (_your name_), command this cancer
to cease all operations in my human body,
Right now,
Cancer leave my body,
Right now,
IN THE NAME OF JESUS.

AUTHORITY- THE DEMONSTRATIONS

THE DEMONSTRATIONS- AUTHORITY OVER CANCER IN THE HUMAN BODY.

Releasing authority to remove cancer in the human body.
1. Ministering, healing and serving into other people's lives.
2. Releasing and making use of your authority to remove cancer out of other people's bodies and lives.
3. [believer's] speak and release my authority for healing in other people's bodies and lives.

BY THE AUTHORITY
INVESTED IN ME,
FATHER,
I command this cancer
In, (   ), body
to be completely healed.
IN THE NAME OF JESUS.
I command cancer in the breast,
brains, colon, prostate, bones
and or any other part of, (   ),
human body to be gone,
Right now,
IN THE NAME OF JESUS.
I stretch forth my hands to you
FATHER,
I give you thanks and praise
for healing in, (   ), human body,
Right now,
IN THE NAME OF JESUS.

AUTHORITY- THE DEMONSTRATIONS

THE DEMONSTRATIONS- AUTHORITY OVER CANCER IN THE HUMAN BODY.

Releasing authority to remove cancer in the human body.
1. Ministering, healing and serving into other people's lives.
2. Releasing and making use of your authority to remove cancer from other people's bodies and lives.
3. [believer's] speak and release your authority for healing in other people's bodies and lives.

IN THE NAME OF JESUS,
I have authority
given to me by God
with this power that
I have the right to use it.
Therefore,
IN THE NAME OF JESUS,
I command the cancer
in, (_his/her name_), body
to leave, (_his/her name_), human body,
Right now,
IN THE NAME OF JESUS.
I'm taking authority
And
I command this, (_the type of cancer_),
cancer to cease all operations
in, (_his/her name_), human body,
Right now,
Cancer- Stop- Go,
Right now,
IN THE NAME OF JESUS.

AUTHORITY- THE DEMONSTRATIONS

THE DEMONSTRATIONS,
Into your life.
Into other people's lives.

Section Eleven
Authority over all the abilities of the enemy

Releasing power and authority to cease Satan and all evils.
1. Ministering, healing and serving into my life.
2. Releasing and exercising my power and authority over all the abilities of the enemy.
3. [self] making use of my authority to seize the adversary temptations.

BY THE AUTHORITY INVESTED IN ME
THROUGH THE PERFECT FINISHED
WORKS OF JESUS CHRIST.
I have authority given to me by God
over all the abilities of the enemy.
IN THE NAME OF JESUS,
with this power and authority.
I command you satan, demon spirits,
evil spirits and all evils to cease
all operations, maneuvers and
temptations against me,
Right now,
IN THE NAME OF JESUS.
By the authority invested in me
I command you satan and all evils to cease
all temptations, get out of my life, leave me now,
be gone- flee, right now.
IN THE NAME OF JESUS.

AUTHORITY- THE DEMONSTRATIONS

THE DEMONSTRATIONS- AUTHORITY OVER ALL THE ABILITIES OF THE ENEMY.

Releasing your power and authority to cease satan and all evils.
1. Ministering, healing and serving into your life.
2. Exercising and releasing your power and authority over all the abilities of the enemy.
3. [self] making use of your authority to seize the temptations of the enemy.

BY THE AUTHORITY INVESTED IN, (_your name_),
THROUGH THE PERFECT
FINISHED WORKS OF JESUS CHRIST.
I, (_your name_), have authority
given to me by God
over all the abilities of the enemy.
IN THE NAME OF JESUS,
with this power and authority
I, (_your name_), command you satan,
demon spirits, evil spirits and all evils
to cease all maneuvers and temptations
Against, (_your name_), and my life,
Right now,
IN THE NAME OF JESUS.
By the authority invested in me
I command you satan and all evils
to cease all temptations,
Get out of my life
be gone- flee,
Right now,
IN THE NAME OF JESUS.

AUTHORITY- THE DEMONSTRATIONS

THE DEMONSTRATIONS- AUTHORITY OVER ALL THE ABILITIES OF THE ENEMY.

Releasing your power and authority to cease satan and all evils.
1. Ministering, healing and serving into your life.
2. Exercising and releasing your power and authority over all the abilities of the enemy.
3. [self] making use of your authority to seize the adversary temptations.

IN THE NAME OF JESUS,
BY THE ALL MIGHTY GOD,
I have been given authority,
I have the authority
and the right to use it.
IN THE NAME OF JESUS,
I command all maneuvers,
operations and temptations
from satan and all evils towards
my family to cease,
Right now
IN THE NAME OF JESUS,
By the authority
invested in me
given to me by God,
I am taking authority,
I am releasing my power,
strength and authority, Right now
IN THE NAME OF JESUS,
I command you satan and all evils
to cease all temptations towards my family,
Get out of my family- lives, Leave my family.
Flee- Go, Right now
IN THE NAME OF JESUS.

AUTHORITY- THE DEMONSTRATIONS

THE DEMONSTRATIONS- AUTHORITY OVER ALL THE ABILITIES OF THE ENEMY.

Release your power and authority to cease satan and all evils.
1. Ministering, healing and serving into your life.
2. Exercising and releasing your power and authority over all the abilities of the enemy.
3. [believer's] making use of your authority to seize the adversary temptations.

I HAVE AUTHORITY
PLACED IN MY
BORNAGAIN SPIRIT BY GOD,
THROUGH THE PERFECT FINISHED
WORKS OF JESUS CHRIST.
I have authority invested in me
IN THE NAME OF JESUS
I am exercising my authority,
I am releasing my authority
And
I command you satan and
all evils to cease all temptations,
maneuvers and operations
towards and or against my family,
friends, neighbors, foes and all
that I know and love,
be gone- flee,
Right now,
IN THE NAME OF JESUS.

AUTHORITY- THE DEMONSTRATIONS

THE DEMONSTRATIONS- AUTHORITY OVER THE ABILITY OF THE ENEMY.

Releasing your power and authority to cease satan and all evils.
1. Ministering, healing and serving into other people's lives.
2. Exercising and releasing your power and authority over all the abilities of the enemy.
3. [believer's] making use of your authority to make a difference in other people's lives.

BY THE AUTHORITY
INVESTED IN ME THROUGH
THE PERFECT FINISHED
WORKS OF JESUS CHRIST.
I have the perfect finished works of
JESUS CHRIST.
I have the power and authority,
IN THE NAME OF JESUS.
Therefore,
I command you satan and all evils
to cease all maneuvers, operations
And temptations on my family, Right now,
IN THE NAME OF JESUS.
I am not asking,
I am taking authority
And
I commanding you satan and all evils
to cease all temptations on my grandparents,
parents, siblings, aunts, uncles, nieces, nephews,
cousins, in-laws, and I, leave my family - be gone,
Right now,
IN THE NAME OF JESUS.

AUTHORITY- THE DEMONSTRATIONS

THE DEMONSTRATIONS- AUTHORITY OVER ALL THE ABILITY OF THE ENEMY.

Releasing your power and authority to cease satan and all evils.
1. Ministering, healing and serving into other people's lives.
2. Exercising and releasing your power and authority over all the abilities of the enemy.
3. [believer's] using your authority to make a difference into other people's lives.

IN THE NAME OF JESUS,
BY THE ALMIGHTY GOD.
I been given authority,
Authority and the right to use it.
IN THE NAME OF JESUS.
I command you satan and all evils
to cease all temptations on the, (___family name/ family tree is name___),
family tree of, (___names of grandparents, parents, children, grandchildrens, great grandchildren and great- great grandchildrens___)
(_____)
(_____)
(_____)
(_____)
(_____)
AND THEIR CHILDREN'S CHILDREN'S,
RIGHT NOW,
LEAVE THE, (___family/ family tree name___),
CEASE AND GO NOW,
IN THE NAME OF JESUS.

Authority, God placed it on every Born again Spirit

Chapter One (1)
"The Knowledge of Rightly Dividing The Lord's Supper"

I Corinthians 11:20- When ye come together therefore into one place, this is not to eat the Lord's Supper.

The holy communion is not like or common like other meals.

11:21- For in eating every one taketh before others his own supper: and one is hungry, and another is drunken.

Rightly dividing the Lord's Supper by knowing the difference between a regular dinner and the Lord's Supper. Divide your regular meal from your communion, The Lord's Supper.

11:22- What? Have ye not houses to eat and drink in? Or despise ye the church of God, and shame them that have not? What shall I say to you? Shall I praise you in this? I praise you not.

The holy communion is not like or common like other meals. Early deaths or dying sick is not because you took communion, it's because you didn't take advantage of the communion. The representation of the bread and the cup, the broken body and the blood of Jesus Christ. Communion, the announcement of Jesus died, died for you.

"The Knowledge of Rightly Dividing The Lord's Supper"

You must understand the context of the word, context is king. Believe and gain the context of how it appears.

I Corinthians 11:23- For I received of the Lord that which also I delivered unto you, That the Lord Jesus the same night in which he was betrayed took bread:
Matthew 26: 26-28
:26- and as they were eating, Jesus took bread, and blessed it, and broke it, and gave it to the disciples, and said, take, eat; this is my body. :27- And he took the cup, and gave thanks, and gave it to them, saying, drink ye all of it; :28- For this is my blood of the new testament, which is shed for many for the remission of sins.
I Corinthians 11:24- And when he had given thanks, he broke it, and said, take, eat: this is my body, which is broken for you: this do in remembrance of me.

   The night Jesus was betrayed, he took the bread, and when he gave thanks, he broke the bread and said- take, eat, this bread is my body- I broke it for you, do this in remembrance of me, remember this bread is my broken body for you, so that any area or part of your body is broken remember my body, this bread is broken for you in remembrance of me.

"The Knowledge of Rightly Dividing The Lord's Supper"

I Corinthians 11:25- After the same manner also he took the cup, when he had supped, saying, This cup is the new testament in my blood: this do ye, as oft as ye drink it, in remembrance of me.
JESUS, The new testament in this cup is my blood, you're already healed and covered by the blood, you already have victory, you're not coming from defeat, you're coming from victory to victory. You were forgiven from all your sins, known and unknown, past, present and future sins. Jesus said: Do this in all thateth you drinketh in remembrance of me. Jesus didn't say remember your sins, he said: in remembrance of me.

Remember, whenever your body is broken remember me so your body can be whole, sound and in peace. Remember when you are taking this cup your body is made sound and in peace. Remember what I did, the sacrifice of my body, the sacrifice of my blood, remind yourself where you are now and where you are no longer.
The New Testament- The New Covenant:
That requires you to believe not your performance.
No works or sacrifice required, only believe in Jesus Christ.
Love, hope, trust, faith and belief in Jesus Christ.

"The Knowledge of Rightly Dividing The Lord's Supper"

I Corinthians 11:26- For as often that you eat this bread, and drink this cup, ye do shew the Lord's death till he comes.

Proclaim John 14:3[Act1:11]

John 14:3- And if I go and prepare a place for you, I will come again, and receive you unto myself; that where I am, there ye may be also.

Acts 1:11- which also said, ye men of Galilee, why stand ye gazing up into heaven? This same Jesus, which is taken up from you into heaven, shall so come in like manner as ye have seen him go into heaven.

Eat this bread, his body is broken for you

Drink this cup, The New Testament in his blood you're announcing the Lord's death until he shows up, come back.

    Everytime you taketh this cup you're announced that the Will is enforced. I'm announcing to you that all my sins have been taken away, I have victory, that Jesus has died and the Will is enforced, that every time I take communion, I'm making the announcement Jesus died, he died, the new testament is alive now.

This is not Supper as you know it.

Believe, take communion and take advantage.

"The Knowledge of Rightly Dividing The Lord's Supper"

I Corinthians 11:27- Wherefore whosoever shall eat this bread and drink this cup of the Lord, unworthily, shall be guilty of the body and blood of the Lord. [John 6:51]
[in an unworthy manner]
John 6:51- I am the living bread which came down from heaven: if any man eats of this bread, he shall live for ever: and the bread that I will give is my flesh, which I will give for the life of the world.

   By eating the bread and drinking from the cup as if it's a regular meal, and not understanding and recognizing what this stands for.

   By eating and drinking it as if it was a snack, instead a body and blood that enforced a new testament.
Instead of recognizing it or doing it unworthily , you're doing it without benefiting from the power of it.

I Corinthians 11:28- But let a man examine himself, and so let him eat of that bread, and drink of that cup.
He is asking you to examine your sins or the meaning of the purpose of what you are doing. Let him examine himself to make sure he is not taking this as a normal or regular meal.

"The Knowledge of Rightly Dividing The Lord's Supper"

HOLY COMMUNION

It's called THE HOLY COMMUNION because it is a meal that is opposite, Holy, sanctified and separate from all meals. This one means something holy in my life. A new testament activated in my life.

Let me examine myself to make sure I'm focused on the bread that represents his broken body, and the blood. The cup that represents the new testament. Make sure you're focused on the sanctification of the holiness of the meal.
If everyone examined themselves for sin, nobody would take communion.
Holiness communion means not like or common like other meals.
I am not COMMON with the world, I've been set aside.
1. When they are broke- I am supplied.
2. When they are sick- I am healed.
3. When they are down- I am full of love, peace, joy and happiness.

"The Knowledge of Rightly Dividing The Lord's Supper"

I am not COMMON with the world, I've been set aside.
1. When they are broke- I am supplied.
2. When they are sick- I am healed.
3. When they are down- I am full of love, peace, joy and happiness.

HOLINESS COMMUNION
Means not like or COMMON like other meals.

I Corinthians 11:29- For he that eateth and drinketh unworthily, eateth and drinketh damnation to himself not discerning the Lord's body.

He that eateth and drinketh as if it is a common meal, not as it is the bread, the broken body of Jesus and the cup, the blood of Jesus, the New Testament in his blood and he eateth and drinketh unworthily.

Not discerning is not knowing the difference between a common meal and holy communion. You are not benefiting yourself because you are not focused on what it means . You have not made the distinction of the holy meal and your supper.

"The Knowledge of Rightly Dividing The Lord's Supper"

I Corinthians 11:30- for this cause many are weak and sick among you, and many sleep.

For you not making the distinction of knowing the difference of this communion then your evening dinner. Many were sick and weak before taking communion. Many are still sick and weak after taking communion, and died early because they didn't recognize the power that grace has given to them. By not recognizing them they continued to be sick and weak.
So,
BY THE BREAD,
The body could not be WHOLE.
BY THE CUP,
Because they did not trust or make a decision to recognize this meal of the broken bread and the body of Jesus and the rest of him.
Many died weak and sickly, early deaths because they had something to strengthen them and they did not recognize that it was not a normal meal. The holy communion, not a normal meal.

"The Knowledge of Rightly Dividing The Lord's Supper"

DIVIDING COMMUNION AND THE REGULAR MEAL

This communion is not for your night dinner. It's been marked for the bread, the body broken for you, the cup that is his blood, the new testament for you, keep announcing that I died until I come for you.

HOLY COMMUNION

You can have communion with a piece of bread and a cup of water.

RECOGNIZING THE BREAD:

Represents the body of Jesus Christ our Lord and Savior.

RECOGNIZING THE CUP:

Represents the New Testament in his BLOOD.

I Corinthians 11:30- for this cause many are weak and sickly among you, and many sleep.

"The Knowledge of Rightly Dividing The Lord's Supper"

ACTIVATE YOUR SPIRITUAL AUTHORITY
JESUS, The savior of our lives.
God gave us two things to represent the savior of our lives.

TONGUE and COMMUNION

Proverbs 18:21- death and life are in the power of the tongue: and they that love it shall eat the fruit thereof.

It is God's power but you have to turn the switch on. It is God's power but you have to activate the authority. God will not violate his word and come and turn the power switch on for you, turn on the power switch and activate your authority.

Activate your spiritual authority. Do not be confused, you're confusing the grace of God Will, with the requirements of the law. Under the law we are not God, but God gave us the authority to act like him to take authority and release authority. Take and release your spiritual authority to shut down your adversaries, cast out demons, heal the sick and raise the dead. Take and release authority, activating your spiritual authority are in the power of the tongue.

"The Knowledge of Rightly Dividing The Lord's Supper"

GOD GAVE US TWO THINGS TO REPRESENT THE SERVICE OF OUR LIVES.
1. TONGUE
2. COMMUNION

TONGUE

Speak it, say it and believe it, know the difference between a regular meal and communion, The Lord's Supper.

The bread represents the broken body of Jesus Christ and in his name I eat wholeness.
And…

This cup is the cup of the New Testament and everything that Jesus has done. I believe, I receive it, right now and I drink it declaring that the New Testament is alive and well in being.

"The Knowledge of Rightly Dividing The Lord's Supper"

COMMUNION

The Lord's Supper, acknowledge and take advantage.

Go ahead, take it and employ it every time you need to announce he died and to look at what you have enforced in your life.

Eateth the bread recognizing the broken body of Jesus Christ our savior and drinketh the cup of Jesus Christ recognizing the blood of Jesus Christ our New Testament.

I Corinthians 11:31- for if we would judge ourselves, we should not be judged.

Judge ourselves, make sure you recognize the distinction (difference) of the lord's supper and a common meal.

I Corinthians 11:32- but when we are judged, we are chastened by the Lord, that we should not be condemned with the world.   [Heb 12:5-10, Rev. 3:19]

"The Knowledge of Rightly Dividing The Lord's Supper"

Hebrew 12: 5- And ye have forgotten the exhortation which speaketh unto you unto children, my son, despise not thou the chastening of the Lord, nor faint when thou art rebuked of him. :6- For whom the Lord loveth he chasteneth, scourgeth every son whom he receiveth. :7-If ye endure chastening, God dealeth with you as with sons;for what son is he whom the father chasteneth not. :8- but if ye be without chastisement, wherefore all are partakers, then are ye bastards, and not sons. :9- Furthermore we have had reverence: shall we not rather be in subjection unto the father of spirit, and live? :10- For they verily for a few days chastened us after their own pleasures; but for our profit, that we might be partakers of this holiness.

Revelations 3: 19- As many as I love, I rebuke and chasten: be zealous therefore, and repent.

"The Knowledge of Rightly Dividing The Lord's Supper"

Revelations 3: 19- As many as I love, I rebuke and chasten: be zealous therefore, and repent.

I Corinthians 11:33- Wherefore, my brethren, when ye come together to eat, tarry one for another.

I Corinthians 11:34- And if any man hunger, let him eat at home; that ye come together unto condemnation. And the rest I will set in order when I come home.

For judgement

HOLINESS COMMUNION
MEANS NOT LIKE OR COMMON LIKE OTHER MEALS

This communion is not about your hunger, regular meal, this communion is about your healing, deliverance, salvation, holiness, the New Testament and his blood, the blood of Jesus Christ.

WHEN YOU'RE AT REST EVERYTHING IS SET IN ORDER.

"The Knowledge of Rightly Dividing The Lord's Supper"

JOHN 6: 53- 58

John 6: 53- Them Jesus said unto them, verily, verily, I say unto you, except ye eat the flesh of the son of man, and drink his blood, ye have no life in you.

John 6: 54- Whoso eateth my flesh, and drinketh my blood, hath eternal life; and I will raise him up at the last day.

John 6: 55- For my flesh is meat indeed, and my blood is drink indeed.

John 6: 56- He that eateth my flesh, and drinketh my blood, dwelleth in me, and I in him.

John 7: 57- As the living Father hath sent me, and I live by the Father: So he that eateth me, even he shall live by me.

John 6: 58- This is that bread which comes down from heaven: not as your Father did eat man- na, and are dead: he that eateth of this bread shall live for ever.

"The Knowledge of Rightly Dividing The Lord's Supper"

THE CONTRAST BETWEEN SUPPER AND THE COMMON TABLE:

THANK YOU JESUS
THANK YOU FATHER
IN THE NAME OF JESUS
FOR THE AUTHORITY

THE AUTHORITY WE RECEIVED AT THE COMMUNION TABLE.
1. Activate this communion in your life.
2. Focus on taking worthily on yourself.
3. Make a distinction
4. Reek the benefits of his broken body and his shedded blood.

YOU AND I WILL NOT:
1. Will not be defeated.
2. Will not stay weak.
3. I will not stay sick.
4. Will not die before your/my time because of what's been invested in the communion.

"The Knowledge of Rightly Dividing The Lord's Supper"

IN THE BOOK OF JOHN, JESUS SAID:
John 6: 51- I am the living bread which came down from heaven: if any man eats of this bread, he shall live for ever: and the bread that I shall give is my flesh, which I will give for the life of the world.
In this book of John, Jesus spoke about communion.
Jesus spoke to the disciples and said:
Drink my blood and eat my flesh and they left the church, thinking he might have them to do so. Jesus said: if you don't you have no part with me, all that he has.
Don't let fear take the place of what you have in communion.
Keep up with it STOP and take COMMUNION
START
Recording all your successes
STOP
Recording your failures
REMEMBER
Jesus left this for us to do and say I'm gone to do it.
Thank you Jesus,
All glory be to God,
And
The Rightly Dividing of The Lord's Supper.

Authority, God placed it on every Born again Spirit

Chapter Two(2)
Spiritual Authority in the midst of a spiritual battle

Ephesians 6:10-19

Ephesians 6:10- Finally, my brethren, be strong- in the Lord, and in the power of his might. :11- Put on the whole armour of God, that ye may be to stand against the wiles of the devil. :12- For we wrestle not against flesh and blood, but against principalities, against powers, against the rulers of the darkness of this world, against spiritual: wickedness in high places. :13- Wherefore take unto you the whole armour of God, that ye may be able to withstand in the evil day, and having done all, to stand. :14- Stand therefore, having your loins girt about with truth, and And your feet shod with the preparation of the gospel of peace; :16- Above all, taking the shield of faith, wherewith ye shall be able to quench all the fiery darts of the wicked. :17- And take the helmet of salvation, and the sword of the spirit, which is the word of God, :18- Praying always with all prayer and supplication in the spirit, and watching thereunto with all perseverance and supplication for all saints; :19- And for me, that utterance may be given unto me, that I may open my mouth boldly, to make known the mystery of the gospel,

Spiritual Authority in the midst of a Spiritual Battle

The issue is there is a battle going on, recognize it, if you don't believe it or recognize it, you'll only look at situations in your life as if it's just simple natural things. When bad things happen in your life, it is a battle going on, spiritual things going on. There is something behind it. The devil has something to do with it. Satan has a plan to destroy you. He wants to steal, kill and destroy your life. Believe and recognize there is a spiritual battle going on and you have spiritual authority. Recognize God has a plan for you. A life of victory, success and prosperity. A life of healing, deliverance and salvation.

Matthew 16:21-23

Matthew 16:21- from that time forth began Jesus to shew unto his disciples, how he must go unto Jerusalem, and suffer many things of the elders and chief priests and scribes and be killed, and he be raised again the third day. :22- then Peter took him, and began to rebuke him, saying, be if far from thee; Lord: This shall not be unto thee. :23- But he turned, and said unto Peter, get thee behind me, Satan: Thou Art an offence unto me: For thou savourest not the things that be of God, but those that be of men.

Spiritual Authority in the midst of a Spiritual Battle

Jesus tells the disciples, tell no man he was Jesus The Christ.

The will of God coming out of the mouth of Jesus The Christ.

He said, I will go to Jerusalem to be sacrificed, and raised three days later.

Jesus looked at Peter but he was speaking to Satan, Peter was being influenced by Satan.

Jesus released his Authority and commanded Satan to get behind him.

Man is the treasure and or reward, between God and Satan. The battle is on, going on.

There is a battle going on between God and Satan, man is the treasure, we are the treasure. You will turn yourself over to God to be influenced or you will turn yourself over to Satan to be influenced.

Jesus recognized Peter was being influenced by Satan. Christian don't recognize there is a spiritual battle going on. We're just limited to recognizing a natural battle going on. Until you recognize that there is a spiritual battle going on, then you're just limited to what it is, what's going on. The devil wants to steal, kill and destroy your life. Turn yourself over to God to be influenced.

GOD WANTS US TO HAVE LIFE MORE ABUNDANTLY

Spiritual Authority in the midst of a Spiritual Battle

Satan will influence you to say things against the will of God, he will influence your attitude, your mind and thoughts (thinking), and he will destroy your life. If you don't realize they're spiritual forces that are trying to destroy your life.

II Timothy 3:12- Yea, and all that will live Godly in Christ Jesus shall suffer persecution.

   Man, all that live Godly, you're gone to suffer persecution. One, you will have run ends with the devil. Secondly, plan on having battles with the devil. Most important, recognize the spiritual battles and use the two things God gave you to represent the savior for our lives, tongue and communion.
   Since I'm gone to suffer persecution and have run ends and battles with the devil, I'm just going to go ahead and do what God wants me to do. I'm gone to recognize the spiritual battles. Take and exercise my spiritual authority and use the two things God gave me to represent the savior for my life, my tongue and communion as often as needed.

Spiritual Authority in the midst of a Spiritual Battle

JESUS SAID:

John 10: 10- The thief cometh not but for to steal, and to kill, and to destroy: I am come that they might have it more abundantly.

   The battle is not natural, it is not luck or fate, it is the devil who is fighting us. Know who your enemy is to be victorious in this battle. Recognize who you are fighting, satan, demon and evil spirits and all the wickedness of the world. If you believe there is no devil, demon and evil spirits, then Satan already got you demonized. Demonizing means Satan is bothering you.
   Christian people can be demonetized by the devil. Your mind and body needs to be renewed, in the word of God. Commit yourself to renew your mind, your mind that's where Satan wants to work. Your mind and thoughts are where Satan wants to influence you, deceive you and lie to you. If you're not in the word and realize there is a battle going on, Satan will be successful with that. Recognize and understand, when things happen, it just doesn't happen. There are spiritual forces that want to protect you, your life. And demonic forces that want to destroy your life.

Spiritual Authority in The midst of a Spiritual Battle

THERE IS A BATTLE GOING ON: HEALTH PROBLEMS

Health problems, they are happening for a reason. Emotional problems, they are happening for a reason. Financial problems, they are happening for a reason. Doctors and scientists will give you a natural reason about your health, emotional and financial problems, and why your life is a mess. Sickness, evil, disease, lack and poverty is in your life instead of healing, deliverance and prosperity.

Satan uses self as one of the en roads to destroy your life. When you are self- centered and think you can do what and when you want. Then you are a puppet for the devil. The devil is destroying you. The devil is your puppet master.

THE CHOICE IS YOURS, WHO YOU CHOOSE?

If you don't choose God then you're choosing by default the devil. If you choose self (self- centered) you're also choosing the devil. Self will send you to hell, it will keep you sick, poor and destroy your life. Deciding to live a life of self, satan got you he loves you to declare self. The choice is yours, who you choose, God, self and or the devil. My choice is God, choose God.

Spiritual Authority in The Midst of a Spiritual Battle

YOUR ACTION HAS SPIRITUAL IMPACT, THERE IS A CONSEQUENCE FOR EVERYTHING YOU DO.

THERE IS A GOD AND THERE IS SATAN AND YOU HAVE TO REALIZE THERE IS A SPIRITUAL BATTLE.

   The grace of God says God loves you in spite of what you do. But it doesn't mean there isn't a consequence in spite of what you do. God doesn't deal with you based on your performance. Satan is waiting to see what you do and how he can influence you and destroy you. God doesn't reject you or punish you, but your actions have consequences and spiritual impact.
   What you do can be empowering the devil to destroy you. By your own authority authorizing Satan to destroy you. If you sin God will not reject you. But your sins will give Satan authority to destroy you, influence and destroy you. Everytime you want to sin, bow down and tell Satan, take possession of me through this sin because this is what you're doing anyway outwardly or not. Everything you do has consequences, exercise your authority in a spiritual battle.

Authority, God placed it on every Born again Spirit
Chapter (3)
Authority of the Believer, Believer's Authority

The Lord shall rise over you and his goodness and kindness will shine on you. Jesus is the true lamb of God that took away our sins.

Every demon in hell sees the blood of Jesus on you. Every demon, satan and all evils sees the armour of authority on you. Every devil in hell sees the authorized uniform that you carry, you have the blood of Jesus on you and every demon recognizes that authority clove with the armour of God. He doesn't know what is behind that armour, it could be Jesus, when you say stop, it stops, satan, demon and evil spirits and all the wickedness of the world.

Speak into existence what you're asking God to do. You have the authority that Jesus already came and did it all. Believers, understand your identity and authority as a believer. God has already spoken on it, you walk in favor. Gospel of grace, that is preached right, hear it, receive it and your faith rises and then prospective changes.

Born again, it is your true identity in Christ. You're blessed, healed, guided and protected in every arena in your life. Don't live by- sight, live by faith, hear the word of God, faith will come by hearing and hearing the word of God.

Authority of The Believer, Believer's Authority

    The bible, the word of God says Satan wants to keep the blind- blind. Satan doesn't want you to know who you are, your true identity.

    God didn't create Lucifer, he didn't create Satan. God does not make mistakes, he doesn't make any mess.

Ezekiel 28:12- 13

Ezekiel 28:12- Son of man, take up a lamentation upon the king Tyrus, and say unto him, thus saith the Lord God; thou sealeth up the sum, full of wisdom and perfect in beauty.

Ezekiel 28:13- Thou has been in Eden the garden of God; every precious stone was thy covering, The sardius, Topaz, and the Diamond, the Beryl, the Onyx and the Jasper, the Sapphire, the Emerald, and the Carbuncle, and Gold: The workmanship of thy tabrets and thy pipes was prepared in thee in the day that thou wast created.

Lucifer was in Eden, The Perfect Garden of God.

Authority of The Believer, Believer's Authority

Revelation 12:4

Revelation 12:4- And his tail drew the third part of the stars of heaven, and did cast theme to the earth: and the dragon stood before the woman which was ready to be delivered, for to devour her child as soon as it was born.

Hebrews 1:14

Hebrews 1:14- Are they not all ministering spirits, sent forth to minister for them who shall be heirs of salvation?

Lucifer was in the garden of Eden to minister to Adam and Eve.
If you're not careful Satan will talk you out of your authority.

II Peter 2:4

II Peter 2:4- for if God spared not the angels that sinned, but cast them down to hell, and delivered them into chains of darkness, to be reserved unto judgement:

   Angels can make a decision to sin, God did not create hell for any man. God created hell for a holding cell, jail for angels who decided to sin. To be revealed, held in jail for time of judgement. Angel was stripped of their authority, conditional and restrictive.

Authority of The Believer, Believer's Authority

WHAT MOTIVATED SATAN TO DO WHAT HE DID?

Lucifer was in the garden of Eden to minister to Adam and Eve. It happened in the garden when he heard and saw that Adam and Eve was given unrestricted and unconditional authority over the whole earth. Man had this authority.

Isaiah 14:13

Isaiah 14:13- For thou hast said in thine heart, I will ascend into heaven, I will exalt my throne above the stars of God: I will sit also upon the mount of the congregation, in the sides of the north:

For you have said in your heart: "I will ascend into heaven, I will exalt my throne above the stars of God; I will also sit on the mount of the congregation on the farthest side of the north; I will ascend above the heights of the clouds, I will be like the most high God".

MAN
Created in God likeness

LUCIFER
Created an arch angel

Authority of The Believer, Believer's Authority

MANEUVERS, OPERATIONS and TEMPTATIONS

LUCIFER, WHAT WAS HE THINKING?

Lucifer was thinking, if I can convince man to submit his authority to me. Then I can be like the most high God because he is turning his authority over to me. Lucifer goes to work, to convince man to turn his authority over to him. Using the body of a serpent to convince Adam and Eve and go after their identity. Adam and Eve gave their authority over to Lucifer. The day man turned their authority over to Lucifer, Lucifer became Satan.

God did not make Satan, man made Satan once they turned over their authority.

Man must understand how powerful you are in authority. When you open your mouth up you give your power of authority to God or Satan. One, God bless you. Second, Satan curses you. You have the power of authority.

Authority of The Believer, Believer's Authority

When God gives you the power and authority, you've got to accept the responsibility. God has to have your cooperation and understanding. He can't intervene when you don't use your authority. You limit God when you don't use your authority. God says I'm for healing, but you have the power. I gave you the power. You have to turn on the authority switch, power switch. Turn on the power, take and release your authority. If God gives you the power, accept the responsibilities. To resist the devil, you've got to resist the devil. To heal the sick, you've got to heal the sick. To get well, you've got to sow a seed. That's how to turn on the authority switch. Authorized by God to use your authority.

Authority is making use of God's power and authority to enforce his word. Get into that word (bible) and discover how things are supposed to be, once you know that it is in the book you'll know how to use your authority to enforce what you just read. Know the nature of God, the will of God for you, God is full of love. He wants good things for you, the word of God, that every man comes to repentance and no man shall never perish.

Authority of The Believer, Believer's Authority

THE HIDDEN GIFT OF GOD

The hidden gift of God, your gift is ready in you for what you're called to do. God's hidden gift is inside of you, it is up to you to put it on display.

TWO EXAMPLES:
MEALS and HOUSES,
ON DISPLAY

THE MEALS:

The meal is in the seed, it's just hidden. You have to sow the seed, harvest and create the meal.

THE HOUSE:

The house is in the tree, it's just hidden. You have to use the technique to turn the trees into a house which becomes your home.

ON DISPLAY: A MEAL IN A HOUSE, YOUR HOME

You have sowed the seed and harvest and created a meal to have and enjoy in the house. You used the technique to turn the trees into a house that is your home.

Authority, God placed it on every Born again Spirit
Chapter four (4)
Christmas Day, The Birth of our Savior
Matthew 1:21- 25

Matthew 1:21- And she brought forth a son, and thou shall call his name JESUS: for he shall save his people from their sins.

Matthew 1:22- Now all this was done, that it might be fulfilled which was spoken of the Lord by the prophet, saying,

Matthew 1:23- Behold, a virgin shall be with child, and shall bring forth a son, and they shall call his name Em- man- uel, which being interpreted is, God with us.

Matthew 1:24- Then Joseph being raised from sleep did as the angel of the Lord had bidden him, and took unto him his wife.

Matthew 1:25- And knew her not till she had brought forth her firstborn son:

SIN NATURE

Sin nature, sin nature will take man to hell. Requirement, it requires someone to come save us from that sin nature. Because of Jesus, who was to be a savior, a savior to deliver man from that sin nature. The significance of Jesus being born, Jesus was born to be the peace offering for man's sins. Peace on earth between God and man sins. Jesus came to save man from sins.

Christmas Day, The Birth of our Savior

Luke 2:8- 14

Luke 2:8- And there were in the same country shepherds abiding in the field, keeping watch over their flock by night.

Luke 2:9- And lo, the angel of the Lord came upon them, and the glory of the Lord shone round about them: and they were sore afraid.

Luke 2:10- And the angel said unto them, fear not: for behold, I bring you good tidings of great joy, which shall be to all people.

Luke 2:11- For unto you is born this day in the city of David a savior, which is Christ the Lord.

Luke 2:12- And this shall be a sign unto you; ye shall find the babe wrapped in swaddling clothes, lying in a manger.

Luke 2:13- And suddenly there was with the angel a multitude of the heavenly most praising God, and saying,

Luke 2:14- Glory to God in the highest, and on earth peace, good will towards men.

Christmas Day, The Birth of a Savior

Eat the bread and drink the cup in remembrance to Jesus. Communion, you can have with a piece of bread and a cup of water.

The bread represents the body of Jesus Christ our Lord Savior.
The cup represents The New Testament in his blood.

St. John 1:29
St. John 1:29- The next day John seeth Jesus coming unto him, and saith, behold the lamb of God, which taketh away the sins of the world.

Behold the man of God, Jesus, who takes (taketh) sins away from the world.

St. John 12:32 [Jesus said]
St. John 12:32- And I, if I be lifted up from the earth, will draw men unto me.

Jesus said, I will draw all man judgement unto me, you didn't deserve it. Whatever judge unto you, Jesus said I'll take it.

Christmas Day, The Birth of a Savior

I John 2:2

I John 2:2- And he is the propitiation for all sins: and not for our's only, but also for the sins of the whole world.

The propitiation for our sins and the whole world, any man.

Hebrew 2:17

Hebrew 2:17- Wherefore in all things it behoved him to be made like unto his brethren, that he might be a merciful and faithful high priest in things pertaining to God, to make reconciliation for the sins of the people.

I John 4:10

I John 4:10- Herein is love, not that we love God, but that he loved us, and sent his son to be the propitiation for our sins.

The propitiation for our sins, he sent his only begotten son to take away our sins. Jesus died for us, he was the perfect sacrifice.

Christmas Day, The Birth of a Savior

AND THINGS TO BE SIGNIFICANT IS TO

WORSHIP JESUS ON CHRISTMAS DAY,

COME BEFORE THE LORD AND OFFER

HIM A GIFT AND WORSHIP GOD.

LET YOUR GIFT WORSHIP AND

REMEMBER HIM.

JESUS,
HE DIED A SAVIOR

JESUS,
BORN A SAVIOR

N GOD RIQ TRUST

GOD LOVED US FIRST WE'RE HIS BELOVED, I TRUST IN GOD'S ABILITY NOT MINE—HIS LOVE.

I HAVE GENUINE HUMILITY, WITH HIS WORDS I PROTECT WHAT IS GRACE TO ME. I'VE READ THE WORD, STUDIED, LEARNED, SPEAK AND MEDITATE. GOD IF YOU SAY SO I'M GONE TO BELIEVE SO. I'M FULLY PERSUADED WITH UNSHAKABLE FAITH. I HAVE THE POWER OF BELIEF AND FAITH IN GOD'S GOODNESS. I'M EXALTED IN GOD RIGHTEOUS AND TRUE HOLINESS. JESUS PAID THE PRICE FOR ALL MEN'S SINS. I'M SAVED BY GRACE, CASE DISMISSED. GLORY BE TO GOD AND THANK YOU JESUS. MY ACCESS IS GRANTED FOR ETERNAL REST IN THE KINGDOM.

THE GOODNESS OF GOD

LEAD ME TO REPENTANCE

NO RESENTMENT

JUST TOTAL COMMENTMENT

BELIEVE AND TRUST

MUST—A—MUST

N GOD—N GOD

N GOD RIQ TRUST

BELIEVE AND TRUST

MUST—A—MUST

N GOD—N GOD

N GOD RIQ TRUST...

R-I-Q TRUST IN GOD

WRITTEN AND DESIGNED BY TAARIQ "R-I-Q" JAAMAL

THE CROSS OF A DISCIPLE

In a Christian context, a disciple is a follower of Jesus Christ who believes in Him, commits to His teaching, strives to become like Him through obedience, and

participates in the mission to spread the gospel. This involves a lifelong spiritual journey of personal growth, worship, service, and witness.

4 MARKS OF A TRUE DISCIPLE

Luke 14:26—if any man come to me, and hate not his father, and mother, and wife, and children, and brethren, and sister, yea, and his own life also, he cannot be my disciple.

Luke 14:33—So likewise, whosoever he be of you that foresaketh not all that he hath, he cannot be my disciple

1. OPEN COMMITMENT TO CHRIST

3. WILLINGNESS TO SACRIFICE

2. OBEDIENCE TO HIS WORD

4. BEARING FRUIT

Luke 9:23—And he said to them all, if any man will come after me, let him deny himself, and take up his cross daily, and follow me.

John 8:31—Then said Jesus to those Jews which believed on him, if ye continue in my word, then are ye my disciples indeed;

John 8:32—And ye shall know the truth, and the truth shall make you free.

Matthew 16:24—Then said Jesus unto the disciples, if any man will come after me, let him deny himself, and take up his cross, and follow me.

Matthew 16:25—For whosoever will save his life shall lose it: and whosoever will lose his life for my sake shall find it.

John 13:34—A new commandment I give unto you, that ye love one another; as I have loved you, that ye also love one another.

John 13:35—by this shall all men know that ye are my disciples, if ye have love one to another.

John 15:16—Ye have not chosen me, but I have chosen you, and ordained you, that ye should go and bring forth fruit, and that your fruit should remain: that whatsoever ye shall ask of the Father in my name, he may give it you.

John 15:17—These things I command you, that ye love one another.